Environmental
Social
Gove

Environmental
Social
Governance

A Framework for the Future of Healthcare

Carla Jackie Sampson, Editor

ACHE Management Series

Library of Congress Cataloging-in-Publication Data
Frontiers of Health Services Management, (ISSN: 0748-8157 [print]), is published quarterly on behalf of the Foundation of the American College of Healthcare Executives by Wolters Kluwer Health, Inc., at 1800 Dual Highway, Suite 201, Hagerstown, MD 21740-6636. Business and production offices are located at Two Commerce Square, 2001 Market St., Philadelphia, PA 19103.

Library of Congress Cataloging-in-Publication Data is on file at the Library of Congress, Washington, DC.
ISBN: 978-1-64055-455-9

Editor of *Frontiers of Health Services Management*: Carla Jackie Sampson; Managing editor: Joe Pixler. Book cover design: Carla M. Nessa; Layout: PerfecType, Nashville, TN.

The paper used in this publication meets the minimum requirements of American National Standard for Information Sciences—Permanence of Paper for Printed Library Materials, ANSI Z39.48-1984. ∞ ™

Found an error or a typo? We want to know! Please e-mail it to hapbooks@ache.org, mentioning the book's title and putting "Book Error" in the subject line.

For photocopying and copyright information, please contact Copyright Clearance Center at www.copyright.com or at (978) 750-8400.

Health Administration Press
A division of the Foundation of the American
   College of Healthcare Executives
300 S. Riverside Plaza, Suite 1900
Chicago, IL 60606-6698
(312) 424-2800

Contents

Part 3: Governance

Case Studies

Introduction

CARLA JACKIE SAMPSON, PHD, MBA, FACHE

Saving our planet, lifting people out of poverty, advancing economic growth . . . these are one and the same fight. We must connect the dots between climate change, water scarcity, energy shortages, global health, food security, and women's empowerment. Solutions to one problem must be solutions for all.

—Ban Ki-moon, former UN Secretary-General,
Address to the 66th General Assembly,
December 2011

HOW CAN HEALTHCARE leaders measure corporate social responsibility and create long-term value for their organizations? As the world faces new waves of existential challenges, the most effective response could be to take an environmental, social, and governance (ESG) approach.

- **Environmental** factors include the responsibility to our planet, including sustainability and resource depletion, pollution, waste management, and climate change.
- **Social** factors hit closer to home and describe local community impact, employee relations, diversity, equity, inclusion, and social justice.
- **Governance** factors involve operational transparency, financial performance, stakeholder engagement, legal

and regulatory compliance, board composition and independence, and risk management.

Today, "ESG" is a mark of progressive leadership in healthcare reframing 20th-century concepts related to how businesses operate in a socially and environmentally responsible manner by adding transparency and accountability (see sidebar). More recently, in corporate governance, the CEO members of the Business Round-table redefined the purpose of the for-profit corporation to include "supporting the communities in which we work." And with that, Wall Street has arrived on healthcare's Main Street. Because most health leaders are seasoned community stewards, they have much to teach other businesses.

Frontiers of Health Services Management, a journal of the American College of Healthcare Executives, published a three-part series on

FROM SOCIAL RESPONSIBILITY TO ESG: LANDMARK CONCEPTS

- **1950s.** Economist Howard R. Bowen suggested that corporations should also pursue objectives aligned with societal values.
- **1970s.** Academician Archie B. Carroll proposed a balance of required corporate actions (economic and legal responsibility) that support expected corporate actions (ethical and philanthropic responsibility).
- **1980s.** Business ethicist R. Edward Freeman presented his stakeholder theory to argue bravely against Milton Friedman's profit-first motive by suggesting that the corporation had a responsibility to every constituent affected by the business operations.
- **1994.** Author and entrepreneur John Elkington's triple bottom line of people, planet, and profits continued this thread of doing good while doing well.

- **2004.** UN Secretary-General Kofi Annan invited financial institutions worldwide to participate in a global compact to foster collective action on social and environmental responsibility.
- **2005.** UN Global Compact Report coins "ESG" to guide the financial sector, including regulators, investors, analysts, business leaders, and academics, in reporting sustainability efforts.

ESG in 2022–2023. Collated, adapted, and expanded for this book, the series reveals overlaps of social conditions and the environment and the role of governance, particularly in its fiduciary and strategic responsibility to prioritize initiatives.

Historically, economic development has come at a disproportionate cost to already vulnerable populations, particularly in the guise of urban development. Health determinants such as clean air, personal safety, walkability, and access to green spaces have been compromised by patterns of built segregation and socioeconomic inequality. The resulting cumulative disadvantage, together with practices that prohibit access to opportunity, produces health outcomes that have more to do with zip code than genetics. There is a broadening public expectation that organizations must measure social impact and include social investments in portfolios.

As the stories in this book illustrate, healthcare organizations are in an excellent position to be a part of the solution as they deliver healthcare beyond their walls.

ENVIRONMENTAL: HEALTHCARE'S LEADING ROLE TO SAVE THE PLANET

First, we explore the context of environmental initiatives. All people can enjoy healthier lives when the organizations dedicated to serving their healthcare needs positively influence their natural surroundings (air, water, and land), built environment, and economic opportunities. Unabated climate change can lead to lives lost, families displaced, food supply disruptions, and severe damage to critical infrastructure—including hospitals. This section takes stock of how the organizations featured in these pages are making strategic choices to take care of our only planet.

SOCIAL: HEALTHCARE'S RESPONSIBILITY FOR EQUITY

Health outcomes become a function of where people live and who they are. Where living conditions decline, residents' health is soon to follow. It is not enough to treat symptoms of inequity. Root causes must be addressed, a point that The Joint Commission underscored with its requirements for health disparities that went into effect in January 2023.

Some may argue that embracing the responsibility for socioeconomic conditions or tackling racism as a public health emergency is mission creep, and that it is a Sisyphean task. However, limiting care only to the treatment of the presenting disease is myopic medicine.

The Affordable Care Act's requirement for community health needs assessments (CHNA) and implementation plans reinforces this responsibility. The challenge is that success will not come overnight even with the best efforts. Lasting success requires commitment from senior leadership, robust community partnerships, and medium- to long-term investments. This section of the book illustrates strategic initiatives that prioritize impact factors beyond care delivery.

GOVERNANCE: THE KEY TO SUSTAINABLE EFFORTS

All the criteria under the ESG framework converge in the third section of this book. Governance sets the direction for the organization, with progress carefully monitored along the way. It is all-encompassing, given the full suite of board responsibilities.

Governance criteria refer to the standards and guidelines organizations use to evaluate and improve their corporate practices, including those that demonstrate their commitment to responsible and sustainable business practices.

The fiduciary responsibility requires that governing boards consider stakeholders who may lack influence but are nonetheless important, such as the poor and disadvantaged. Productive boards are progressive and include the perspectives of members who advocate for an overlooked issue—they help to generate and refine new strategies to thrive in a modern value-based healthcare model.

The business of governance is given special attention in an additional chapter written for this book (181–92). ESG risks can have a significant impact on an organization's performance. These less-obvious risks can be related to climate change, basic human rights, and social equity. Boards can help protect their organizations' operations and financial performance by recognizing and managing these risks and promoting sustainable and responsible business practices to address them.

HOPE FOR THE FUTURE

This book is primarily intended to engage and inspire today's healthcare leaders. Each chapter ends with a set of questions to spur thought and discussion in the workplace. But I have found that future healthcare leaders can find plenty to think about and talk about here as well.

In teaching a course in health management and strategy at New York University's Robert F. Wagner Graduate School of Public Service, I have adapted the midterm group project to incorporate the ESG journey. My graduate students critique a community health needs assessment (CHNA) from the local market, given what they've learned about the social determinants of health. They typically question the check-the-box implementation plans that appear to leave pressing community needs unmet. They examine an organization and its stated strategies using the MacMillan Matrix to determine whether it effectively identifies and manages risks related to environmental, social, and governance issues. They explore whether an approach fits the organization's guiding statements, experience, and strategic initiatives. They parse whether the opportunity is economically attractive by considering the effect on reimbursement or net assets, market demand, and the chance to attract new revenue. They also consider how the organization will measure the outcomes to determine the impact on the at-risk population.

Over the five years that I have taught similar classes, their angry dismissal of rote CHNA implementation plans (*Oh great, "culturally appropriate" services!*) has been replaced by optimism and new energy (*This health system is focused on social services, but how does this affect operations now and in the future?*). This shift in thinking reflects the trend of healthcare organizations telling better stories about their social and environmental initiatives and being more transparent about their measures—inspiring stories like those shared in this book.

I continue to be buoyed by the creativity and design thinking that come naturally to the next generation. They are willing to challenge the status quo enthusiastically, primarily to address health inequity. Today's healthcare leaders are wise to take note. As Michael J. Dowling, president and CEO of Northwell Health, notes in his contribution to this book, this next generation will carefully examine an organization's mission, brand, and social impact to determine whether it is a place where they would want to work.

> For specific tips on academic applications for this book, see "Suggested Uses in the Classroom," page 247.

The Environment

Climate Change and Healthcare:
A Complicated Relationship

KATHY GERWIG, MBA

SUMMARY

Climate change is a crisis with a devastating impact on health. The warming atmosphere is increasing the tolls of deaths and illnesses from heat waves, extreme weather, poor air quality, insect-borne diseases, and other conditions. Healthcare is connected to climate change in a way that is not fully appreciated by many healthcare leaders—in fact, the sector generates a significant share of greenhouse gas emissions that cause climate change. As additional costs, healthcare providers' margins are put at risk from treating more climate-related diseases and illnesses, supply chain disruptions, and damage from severe storms and wildfires. These connections provide a compelling rationale for healthcare executives to create more resilience in operations, lead efforts toward decarbonization, and catalyze climate action.

A WILDFIRE IN northern California jumps from a forest into a city, forcing a hospital to close. A superstorm hits the East Coast, causing evacuations of 6,300 patients in New York City. A heat wave blasts the Pacific Northwest with temperatures of 110 degrees, costing the lives of hundreds of mostly poor and elderly people.

These recent devastating events have something in common: their association with the climate crisis. In response, meaningful actions to reduce greenhouse gas emissions must be accelerated to avoid the worst human health consequences of global warming because the human toll from inaction is real and worsening.

The United Nations warns that global emissions must be cut in half by 2030 and get to zero by 2050 to keep warming to 1.5 degrees Celsius (2.7 degrees Fahrenheit) and avoid the most catastrophic effects of climate change (Intergovernmental Panel on Climate Change 2022). Healthcare has an outsized role to play in achieving this imperative. The sector both contributes to and is burdened by the implications of this health crisis, and it is in a unique position to speed up solutions.

CLIMATE CHANGE AND HEALTH

Health concerns are front and center in the climate crisis, and the harms are widely recognized. Two overarching effects make climate change a health crisis:

1. The warming trend supercharges the frequency and severity of weather disasters across the planet, which leads to injury, death, displacement, and damage to property and ecosystems.
2. Health consequences are especially devastating for people with higher existing health risks, especially older adults, children, those with chronic conditions or disabilities, and those living in low-income communities or communities of color.

Climate change affects health in many ways. Some examples follow.

- **Heat.** As the deadliest result, heat waves occur more frequently and last longer without sufficient cooling at night.
- **Air quality.** Worsened by warmer weather and wildfire smoke, poor air quality causes respiratory illnesses such as asthma.
- **Severe weather.** Superstorms, floods, long-term droughts, and destructive winds wreak widespread injury, death, and destruction.
- **Vector-borne illnesses.** As mosquitoes and other insects thrive at expanded latitudes and elevations, more people are exposed to Lyme disease, malaria, and dengue fever.
- **Food and water contamination.** Pathogens such as salmonella occur more frequently with persistently high temperatures and rainfall—prime conditions for diarrhea and other diseases.
- **Food scarcity.** Droughts and severe weather strike at crop production, resulting in hunger, malnutrition, and population displacement.
- **Mental health trauma.** Severe weather events and heat waves are associated with immediate trauma as well as with longer-term despair resulting from a suddenly uncertain future (U.S. Global Change Research Program 2016).

CLIMATE CHANGE AND HEALTHCARE DELIVERY

We're Part of the Problem

Many leaders in care delivery are surprised to learn that their operations contribute significantly to a warming climate. If the global health sector were a country, it would be the fifth largest emitter of greenhouse gases in the world (Arup and Health Care Without Harm 2019); in the United States, 8.5 percent of emissions are from healthcare (Dzau et al. 2021).

Some important sources of emissions can be controlled through operations. These include the consumption of natural gas to heat and cool buildings, anesthetic and medical gases, fleet vehicles fuel, refrigerants, and purchased electricity. Such uses typically account for about 20 percent of all emissions for a healthcare organization. The rest results from decisions each organization makes that are indirectly tied to emissions through its supply chain and investments. For example, if a computer you purchase was made with coal-fired energy, it has a larger carbon footprint than one made with renewable energy. Investments you make in fossil-fuel holdings exert a larger footprint, as well. Other indirect emission sources to consider include staff commutes, business travel, patient transportation, contracted deliveries, waste disposal, and leased assets.

Where Healthcare Feels Burdens of Climate Change

Infrastructure

Hard lessons were learned in 2005 from Hurricane Katrina when hospitals were flooded and their basement mechanical plants stopped functioning, which led to patient deaths. Now, power systems are more commonly located at elevated levels. In 2017, the wildfire that shut down a northern California hospital forced an emergency evacuation, and it remained closed for more than two weeks while all supplies could be replaced and the facility cleared of smoke. Today, huge wildfires are regular occurrences in the United States, prompting hospitals to enhance their emergency plans and infrastructure to better anticipate and respond to the growing risk.

Among specific infrastructure risks of severe storms, sea-level rise and coastal erosion, and wildfires are:

- suspension or closure of key facilities (clinical, research, information technology),
- compromised ventilation as a result of harm to energy and mechanical systems,

- damaged property,
- release of hazardous material,
- undermined availability and quality of water,
- interrupted supply chains, and
- inaccessible roadways.

Hospitals in regions that are most at risk are investing in resilience by hardening their buildings' facades and equipment against wind and flood damage, relocating critical infrastructure and clinical services above flood and storm surge levels, building barriers to mitigate storm surge intensity, and expanding on-site generator capacity.

Financial Cost
In addition to the infrastructure costs from climate-exacerbated severe weather and wildfires, the health costs of fossil fuel–related air pollution total $820 billion per year in the United States (De Alwis and Limaye 2021). Medical treatment for health problems worsened by climate change is expensive and a financial burden to patients, employers, public and private insurers, and health system operators.

Supply Chain Disruption
Hurricane Maria devastated Puerto Rico in 2017, shutting a major production facility for saline intravenous bags. The subsequent shortage of these ubiquitous medical products throughout the US healthcare system lasted for months. The COVID-19 pandemic also has exposed vulnerabilities in the healthcare supply chain that will worsen the impact of climate change on the production and delivery of supplies, medicine, and equipment.

Investor Concerns
In April 2022, the Securities and Exchange Commission proposed a rule (87 FR 21334) that would require publicly traded companies to disclose their climate-related risks and greenhouse gas emissions to investors. Investors have been stepping up their demands to understand the financial risks related to climate change, and this pressure

is causing companies to create more robust plans to reduce their greenhouse gas emissions.

Impact on Personnel

Healthcare leaders are very concerned about burnout and staffing shortages. Climate change adds to those vulnerabilities. The California wildfire mentioned earlier had a catastrophic impact on the hospital staff, as hundreds of employees and physicians lost their homes. These individuals were both caregivers and victims of the disaster. The trauma they experienced is repeated in every community that suffers from extreme storms, deadly heat waves, and wildfires. Experiencing these types of events can cause significant distress and contribute to more serious mental health issues such as anxiety disorders and depression.

THE BENEFITS OF CLIMATE-SMART ACTIONS

Healthcare executives should consider the financial benefits that can be derived from their leadership in reducing greenhouse gas emissions. Some examples follow.

- **Lower costs.** Optimizing energy systems, reducing water consumption, and adopting other green building features can lower energy and operating costs.
- **Energy price stability.** Drawing from renewable energy sources, on-site and off-site, can help stabilize prices.
- **Ongoing value.** Reducing waste reduces the expenses of disposal and emissions.
- **Less damage.** Designing resilient facilities can result in lower damage costs from extreme weather and wildfires.
- **Staff recruitment and retention.** Attracting and keeping talent is easier, as many health professionals today prefer to work where climate change action is a priority.

- **Risk avoidance.** Avoiding loss of value associated with risks that are not adequately addressed is especially important to investor-owned organizations.
- **Cleaner air.** Reducing air pollution from fossil fuel use mitigates health risks and saves lives.

HOW TO LEAD THE BATTLE

There are several strategic commitments that healthcare executives can make now to ensure a healthier future for their organizations and their communities.

Set a Target of Zero Emissions

- Set targets to cut emissions in half by 2030 and achieve zero emissions by 2050 (as suggested by Science Based Targets at https://sciencebasedtargets.org/). While the work presents challenges, the crucial importance of this goal is commensurate with the health crisis associated with climate change.

Understand Your Emissions

- Conduct an inventory of emissions from facility operations and purchased energy using the Greenhouse Gas Protocol (see https://ghgprotocol.org/corporate-standard).
- Conduct a spend-based inventory for those emissions you influence through your supply chain and investment portfolios, and calculate other activities such as commuting, business travel, and so forth (as outlined by the EPA Center for Corporate Climate Leadership at https://www.epa.gov/climateleadership/scope-3-inventory-guidance).

Prepare and Execute a Reduction Plan

Reduce Emissions You Control

- Cut facility energy use through efficiency and design initiatives. The US Green Building Council's LEED certifications (posted at https://www.usgbc.org/leed) specify actions for new and existing buildings.
- Invest in renewable energy through on-site and off-site solar and wind installations.
- Reduce natural gas used for heating and cooling buildings by transitioning to renewable energy modes such as geothermal, hydrogen, and biomass.
- Purchase zero-emissions fleet vehicles.
- Switch to lower-emission anesthetic gases (e.g., eliminate the use of desflurane), consider waste anesthetic gas–capturing systems, and reduce nitrous oxide waste—especially from centrally piped systems.

Reduce Emissions You Influence

- Encourage suppliers to reduce their operational emissions over which they have direct control (i.e., emissions related to buildings, fleets, purchased energy).
- Limit waste by minimizing the use of single-use devices and plastics and implementing circular systems in which materials have lasting value when maintained through repair and recapture.
- Decrease business travel by continuing the pandemic-induced practice of virtual meetings.
- Incentivize staff commuting by public transit, walking, and bicycling; optimize remote work.
- Reduce patient and visitor trips through transit shuttles and by consolidating patient appointments with multiple providers.

- Promote local and seasonal meal menus while reducing reliance on resource-intensive meat and dairy products.

Link Climate and Quality Initiatives
- Prioritize high-quality, high-value healthcare and promote preventive care to avoid illnesses while reducing healthcare costs and emissions associated with treating (and re-treating) diseases.
- Cut inefficient and unnecessary practices.
- Reduce unnecessary pharmaceutical use.
- Include greenhouse gas emissions data on leadership and quality performance dashboards.

CONCLUSION

Greenhouse gas emissions must be eliminated to avoid the most catastrophic effects of climate change that are already underway. Healthcare leaders must address the sector's greenhouse gas footprint, which is a sizable portion of the entire US footprint. Decarbonization strategies can yield benefits such as reduced financial and operational risks and infrastructure resilience. Healthcare executives can leverage their roles as community leaders by acting with urgency. The way out of this health crisis is for healthcare organizations and their global value chains to be catalysts for a carbon-free future.

ADDITIONAL RESOURCES

Gerwig, K. 2014. *Greening Health Care: How Hospitals Can Heal the Planet.* Oxford University Press. https://doi.org/10.1093/med/9780199385836.001.0001.

Health Care Without Harm. 2018. "Safe Haven in the Storm: Protecting Lives and Margins with Climate-Smart Health

Care." Accessed July 21, 2022. https://noharm-uscanada.org
/safehaven.

———. 2021. "Race to Zero Campaign for Health Care." Accessed
July 21, 2022. https://healthcareclimateaction.org/racetozero.

MacNeill, A. J., H. Hopf, A. Khanuja, S. Alizamir, M. Bilec, M. J.
Eckelman, L. Hernandez, F. McGain, K. Simonsen, C. Thiel, S.
Young, R. Lagasse, and J. D. Sherman. 2020. Transforming the
Medical Device Industry: Road Map to a Circular Economy."
Health Affairs 39 (12): 2088–2097. https://doi.org/10.1377
/hlthaff.2020.01118.

World Health Organization. 2021. "Climate Change and Health."
Accessed July 21, 2022. https://www.who.int/news-room/fact
-sheets/detail/climate-change-andhealth.

REFERENCES

Arup and Health Care Without Harm. 2019. "Healthcare's
Climate Footprint." Accessed July 15, 2022. https://www
.arup.com/perspectives/publications/research/section
/healthcaresclimate-footprint.

De Alwis, D., and V. S. Limaye. 2021. "The Costs of Inaction: The
Economic Burden of Fossil Fuels and Climate Change on Health
in the United States." Accessed July 15, 2022. https://www.nrdc
.org/sites/default/files/costsinaction-burden-health-report.pdf.

Dzau, V. J., R. Levine, G. A. Barrett, and A. Witty. 2021. "Decarbon-
izing the U.S. Health Sector—A Call to Action." *New England
Journal of Medicine 385* (23): 2117–2119. https://doi.org/10.1056
/NEJMp2115675.

Intergovernmental Panel on Climate Change. 2022. "IPCC Sixth
Assessment Report: Impacts, Adaptation and Vulnerability."
Accessed July 15, 2022. https://www.ipcc.ch/report/ar6/wg2//.

U.S. Global Change Research Program. 2016. "The Impacts of Climate Change on Human Health in the United States: A Scientific Assessment." Accessed July 15, 2022. http://health2016 .globalchange.gov/.

PRACTICE GREENHEALTH: A SUPPORT SYSTEM FOR SUSTAINABILITY

Practice Greenhealth is a networking organization of more than 1,500 US and Canadian hospitals and healthcare systems. Together, they embrace sustainability to practice the Hippocratic oath's ethical precepts—to heal and to do no harm—through emissions reduction, elimination of toxic chemicals and products, creation of safer working environments, waste reduction, healthier food offerings, and more efficient use of energy and water.

Representing 20 percent of the US economy with a workforce of 22 million, healthcare has the power to transform lives, communities, and markets. To help its members do that, Practice Greenhealth provides information, tools, data, resources, and expert technical support for local sustainability initiatives. When tied to business and mission-driven goals, sustainability programs yield benefits not only for the planet but also for a hospital's financial bottom line, patient satisfaction and well-being, employee engagement, and the communities healthcare organizations serve.

Reducing Wastes, Reducing Costs

Over the past seven years, Practice Greenhealth member hospitals have achieved remarkable results: 1.5 million kilowatt hours of energy saved through energy efficiency, 1.8 million metric tons of carbon avoided through mitigation and resilience, 424,000 metric tons of carbon avoided through the use of renewable energy, 1.5 billion gallons of water saved, and 1.9 billion pounds of waste diverted from landfills. In addition, these projects have reduced operational costs. Savings have ranged from approximately $200,000 annually at a small critical access hospital to more than $5.5 million in 2019 at a large academic medical center. Annual savings across the membership have averaged around $350,000 on waste-related costs, $214,000 through advancements in energy efficiency, and $300,000 by implementing Practice Greenhealth's operating room strategies.

In sum, these results help organizations understand the cost, impact, and performance of their past and present sustainability initiatives and anticipate future conditions and requirements, allowing them to unlock hidden value and build more resilient enterprises.

Practice Greenhealth's tools help hospitals and health systems measure sustainability metrics, identify gaps, refine goals, and focus their sustainability efforts. Individualized sustainability report cards provide an annual snapshot of a facility's performance on 30 metrics along with percentile comparisons to peer hospitals. Also, the annual *Sustainability Benchmark Report* covers industry statistics, trends, and emerging issues.

Celebrating Achievements

Practice Greenhealth goes beyond benchmarking and annually celebrates sustainability achievements through its Environmental Excellence Awards program. Stony Brook University Hospital, a long-standing member, has consistently been recognized for its environmental sustainability leadership, most recently receiving Practice Greenhealth's Top 25 Environmental Excellence Award. A culture of sustainability is embedded into its public-facing environmental commitments, sustainability grand round series for staff and leadership, and meticulous practices in data collection and review. Gap analyses help SBUH recognize needs and strategize new ways to reduce insulin, pharmaceutical waste, and other chemicals.

Another leader in environmental sustainability, Ascension has aligned its sustainability efforts in areas that have the greatest impact, including sustainable procurement, green building, and waste reduction. The health system applies Practice Greenhealth's data collection framework to its annual reporting and goal-setting for its environmental stewardship program. Ascension's commitment to net-zero carbon emissions and zero waste by 2040 serves as an inspiration for other health systems to set ambitious sustainability goals.

As a network of like-minded organizations, Practice Greenhealth hospitals and health systems participate in work groups through virtual cohort calls. Cohorts are groups of sustainability and healthcare professionals of similar regions, interests, and hospital types from children's hospitals to academic medical centers. They meet to learn from peers and experts, develop strategies to overcome barriers to sustainability progress, and expand their network with new connections to leaders and innovators.

Participants say that they benefit from the successes and experiences of colleagues across the country, implementation guidance from experts, and the resources and tools that are appropriate to where they are in their sustainability journey.

Practice Greenhealth

FOR DISCUSSION

1. Considering the many ways climate change affects health, what is the most significant environmental concern in your community?
2. Which are some of the standard operations at your institution that contribute to greenhouse gas emissions?
3. What climate-smart actions could you recommend to your institution? How would you make a business case for their adoption?
4. How can climate initiatives support quality initiatives over both the short and long term?

A Faith-Based Healthcare Organization Turns the Tide of Environmental Impact

CRAIG A. CORDOLA, MBA, MHA, FACHE

SUMMARY

The healthcare sector's role in every community is inextricably linked to the health of those it serves. As research and media reports point to the significant impact of people on our planet's ecosystems, Ascension has responded by setting several environmental sustainability goals. Our work is defined by three pillars:

- **Net Zero Places** focuses on carbon sources associated with Ascension's physical environments—carbon footprint, operational efficiency of facilities, and sustainable transportation.
- **Responsible Supply Chain** focuses on the flow of goods from procurement to disposition—responsible purchasing, product usage management, recycling, and waste management.
- **Healthy Communities** focuses on the relationship between sustainability and social determinants of

health (SDOH)—linking determinants to Ascension's mission to sustain and improve the health of those we serve, especially the poor and vulnerable.

When we think about future generations, we realize that this work cannot wait. That is why we are reimagining today what environmental impact and sustainability could look like through the next decade and beyond. We are setting our corporate sights on net zero carbon and zero waste by 2040 and encourage other healthcare organizations to join us in these efforts. Working together, we can make a difference.

ENVIRONMENTAL CONSCIENTIOUSNESS HAS come to the forefront of public interest this past decade, but what drove one of the largest healthcare organizations in the United States to take action by setting bold goals such as net zero carbon and zero waste, and what do the strategies to achieve them look like?

Ascension is a nonprofit healthcare system dedicated to transformation through innovation across the continuum of care. More than 150,000 associates and 40,000 aligned providers work at more than 2,600 sites of care, including hospitals and senior living facilities in 19 states and the District of Columbia. In addition to clinical and network services, Ascension provides venture capital investing, investment management, biomedical engineering, facilities management, and risk management, as well as contracting through a group purchasing organization.

As a healthcare ministry, Ascension sees the commitment to environmental sustainability as both an expectation and an opportunity to approach our work differently, because healthcare's impact on the environment is inextricably linked to the health of the communities and patients in our care—and not always in a good way. For example, US greenhouse gas emissions from healthcare represent an incredible 10 percent of *all* US emissions (Hogan 2022). We are a part of the problem.

Climate effects have already riddled many of the communities Ascension serves. Extreme heat days have become more common in Austin, Texas. Places such as Nashville, Tennessee, have experienced frequent and intense rain events due to increased atmospheric temperatures. As oceans absorb heat, hurricane seasons are starting earlier and becoming more severe, as seen in our communities from Mobile, Alabama, to Jacksonville, Florida.

Ascension is committed to taking a greater role in sustainability. Because waste and energy management are areas where we can have the biggest and most tangible influence, this commitment will in turn make a positive impact on the communities we serve. Considering our system's broad scale and scope, we are leveraging all we know about health and healthcare to address these growing needs.

RESPONSE: A LONG-TERM PROGRAM

To establish a path forward, Ascension developed a long-term environmental impact and sustainability program built upon existing efforts in energy conservation, waste management, recycling, environmentally preferred purchasing, and the use of renewable energy. With the guidance of senior leaders, as well as internal and external subject matter experts, Ascension developed the following purpose statement to guide our work:

> Ascension's commitment to reducing our environmental impact and achieving sustainability is rooted in our mission, which calls us to be advocates for a compassionate and just society in our actions and our words. Through Catholic social teaching, we recognize the human dignity of all people and the common good as we work toward

equitable access to resources to improve community health and the lives of the individuals we serve.

Our leaders and associates are working across our markets to improve the efficiency, resiliency, and sustainability of our practices. This sharpened focus is the result of a yearlong effort to develop a sustainability strategy that maximizes environmental benefits for decades to come. The program's activities support the three pillars that are depicted in Exhibit 1 and described in the following sections.

Exhibit 1: Three Pillars of Work

Net zero places
- Energy efficiency
- Renewable energy
- Mobility

Responsible supply chain
- Sourcing
- Waste

Healthy communities
- Partnerships
- Community engagement
- Public policy

Source: Ascension and ENGIE Impact. Copyright 2021 Ascension, St. Louis, Missouri. All permission requests for this image should be made to the copyright holder.

NET ZERO PLACES

This work is centered on carbon sources associated with our physical environments—energy, water, and mobility (fleet vehicles as well as associate, patient, and visitor transportation to and from sites of care). Water and energy are managed together because every step of the water cycle consumes energy. This pillar considers the carbon footprint and operational efficiency of our facilities as well as our transportation channels.

Our FY 2021–2023 goal sets a 5 percent reduction in greenhouse gas emissions from our 2020 baseline. We want to reduce energy consumption and make the transition to clean energy sources to reduce air pollution. To achieve this near-term goal, investments are being made in energy-efficient capital and operations projects. We are shifting to renewable energy sources and electrifying gas-powered landscape equipment and fleet vehicles. The ultimate goal is net zero carbon emissions by 2040.

RESPONSIBLE SUPPLY CHAIN

Supply chain responsibility work encompasses the flow of goods from their procurement through disposition after use. These efforts are intended to ensure that we buy only what we need and practice responsible sourcing and disposal of what we buy. As a result, we lower environmental impact, provide social good, and move in the direction of a circular economy in which material use is reduced and waste is recaptured to create new materials.

Ascension also seeks to create and support a cost-effective value chain that accelerates change toward a value-based care model. This approach is in alignment with our commitment to holistic care for the individual and the common good as well as to Catholic social teaching. We are embracing a tremendous opportunity to change our work in supply chain management of what comes in and out of our facilities while we also minimize the footprint that we leave behind.

Our FY 2021–2023 goal involves reducing municipal solid waste that is sent to landfills by 6 percent from our 2019 baseline. This will cut landfill use in our communities and the emissions from those landfills. Ascension is working to prevent waste by right-sizing purchases, increasing single-stream and cardboard recycling programs, and installing food waste digesters. The plan is to recycle half of the nonhazardous waste from all managed facilities by 2030 and achieve zero waste by 2040.

HEALTHY COMMUNITIES

While most of the work at Ascension has focused on realizing energy savings and thinking differently about how we acquire and run our facilities, making a difference in the health and well-being of the people in our communities, particularly the poor and vulnerable, is at the heart of our environmental impact and sustainability program.

Going a step further to address the SDOH, we realize that climate change and severe weather events have greater consequences for the disadvantaged. As we advance our environmental efforts, we can make a significant positive impact on the health of our communities, as shown in Exhibit 2.

We are examining the SDOH so that we can design programs with clinical interventions that create healthier environments. We want to work closely with the individuals and communities most affected by climate change to improve their lives and livelihood. Other intended outcomes include healthier communities, greater patient comfort, and enhanced patient safety (as illustrated in Exhibit 2). This approach comprises stakeholder and partner identification; data requirements; community engagement; development of shared objectives; and identification of local, state, and federal government policies. The anchor mission approach for healthcare leverages our business practices around inclusive local hiring and workforce development, diverse local sourcing, and local investment. In taking this approach, we can tackle underlying causes of poor health by advancing the social and economic well-being of the communities we serve.

GOVERNANCE

We are fortunate at Ascension to have full support from our board, sponsor, and senior leadership for these initiatives. The governance structure of the environmental impact and sustainability program

Exhibit 2: Climate Change Impact on the Poor and Vulnerable

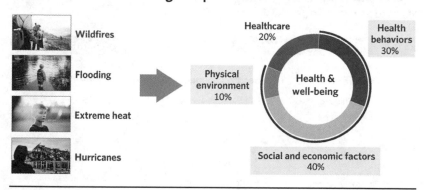

Source: Ascension and ENGIE Impact. Copyright 2021 Ascension, St. Louis, Missouri. All permission requests for this image should be made to the copyright holder.

Note: Data from County Health Rankings (www.countyhealthrankings.org /our-approach) and American Hospital Association (www.aha.org/social -determinantshealth/populationcommunity-health/community-partnerships).

extends from an executive steering committee to green teams at most sites of care. The steering committee guides the strategy and includes leaders from Ascension; Medxcel, our facilities management organization; and The Resource Group, our group-purchasing organization. The environmental impact office is made up of interdependent, cross-functional working groups with executive sponsors and sustainability leads to drive implementation and resource deployment consistent with the three pillars. Green teams at the sites of care drive green practices to create a continuum of engagement for Ascension associates. Exhibit 3 depicts the governance structure.

SUCCESS STORIES

The environmental impact and sustainability program is essentially new for Ascension, but it is also a continuation of work that began in 2008. Exhibit 4 shows the environmental journey and milestones.

Exhibit 3: Ascension's Environmental Impact and Sustainability Governance Model

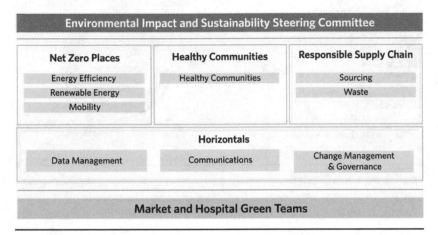

Source: Ascension. Copyright 2021 Ascension, St. Louis, Missouri. All permission requests for this image should be made to the copyright holder.

We have taken a fresh look at Ascension's sustainability initiatives to mitigate the effects of climate change, expand and enhance "green thinking" across the organization, and improve our communities. Following are selected reports of our successes with various organizations that we are working with to support the implementation of our strategies.

Green Teams

Ascension's sustainability efforts have largely rested on the contributions of green teams at each site of care made up of a cross-functional group of associates who are interested in achieving sustainability. Green teams report on energy and water consumption and waste management for their facility or market. They also celebrate significant environmental events such as Earth Day and the Feast of Saint Francis with projects tailored to each ministry throughout the year.

Exhibit 4: Ascension's Environmental Journey and Milestones

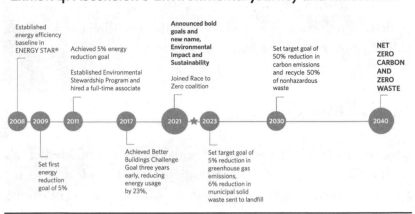

Source: Ascension. Copyright 2021 Ascension, St. Louis, Missouri. All permission requests for this image should be made to the copyright holder.

Department of Energy Better Buildings Challenge

After meeting an initial goal to reduce energy use by 5 percent in 2011, Ascension committed to a 20 percent reduction by 2020, as outlined by the US Department of Energy's Better Buildings Challenge (https://betterbuildingssolutioncenter.energy.gov/challenge/about). From July 2008 to June 2017, Ascension cut energy use by 23 percent, achieved $53.3 million in cost avoidance, and averted more than 1.1 million tons of carbon dioxide emissions across an acute care hospital portfolio of 35 million square feet. From July 2017 to June 2021, Ascension achieved an additional 8.6 percent reduction in energy costs and $42.7 million in energy cost avoidance across a 48.1-million-square-foot acute care hospital portfolio.

Race to Zero

Ascension committed to the United Nation's Race to Zero campaign in October 2021 (https://unfccc.int/climate-action/race-to-zero -campaign). This global coalition is charged with achieving net zero carbon emissions by 2050. Ascension aims to achieve this goal by 2040 and is currently developing science-based interim targets: a 50 percent reduction of scope 1 and 2 emissions (direct and indirect emissions over which we have control) by 2030.

Supply Chain Sustainability

Ascension participates in the National Academy of Medicine's Action Collaborative on Decarbonizing the US Health Sector and the Health Care Supply Chain and Infrastructure Working Group (http://amdr.org/2022/04/national-academy-ofmedicine -action-collaborative-ondecarbonizing-the-u-s-health-sectorvirtual -meeting/). We work with vendors to influence supplier behavior regarding sustainability.

Waste Diversion

Food waste resulting from preparation, overproduction, and leftovers can account for up to 15 percent of Ascension's total solid waste sent to municipal landfills. To address this problem, Medxcel, in cooperation with The Resource Group and TouchPoint Support Services (Ascension's food and nutrition services provider), led a three-month food digester pilot study at Ascension St. Vincent's Riverside in Florida and Ascension Saint Agnes in Baltimore to determine whether the mechanical composting technology would work at other Ascension hospitals. By the conclusion of the 12-week pilots, 32 tons of food waste were diverted from landfills and instead became gray water (uncontaminated with sewage). Installation of 60 digesters across Ascension got underway in 2022. Based on pilot data, more than 3,400 tons of food waste will be digested and diverted from landfills per year.

A Circular Economy

The Resource Group has led the way to reprocess and recycle single-use devices under a program developed by the US Food and Drug Administration. This initiative reduces waste sent to landfills and lowers expenses. Single-use devices are collected and sent to reprocessing centers to be cleaned, recalibrated, repackaged, and sterilized for reuse. In 2021, Ascension hospitals collected more than 1.1 million devices, resulting in 481,000 pounds of waste diverted from landfills and more than $19 million in savings to purchasers of the recycled/discounted devices. Since the program began in 2013, more than 4.9 million pounds of waste have been diverted from landfills.

Another significant initiative that began in late 2021 is the reuse of existing equipment throughout the system. In the first 10 months, we reallocated more than 989 devices systemwide, such as beds, monitors, C-arms, linear accelerators, pumps, and mobile X-ray systems. The estimated replacement cost avoidance exceeds $12 million.

Antibiotic-Free Food

Ascension has participated in the Less Meat, Better Meat health systems collaboration led by Practice Greenhealth (https://practice greenhealth.org/). We worked with our food and nutrition services partner as well as our infection control team to purchase meatless meal options and poultry raised without the use of antibiotics. By aligning with other health systems to change the markets, we helped support the availability of this food.

APPLICATIONS OF LESSONS LEARNED

While our long-term environmental impact and sustainability program has achieved significant momentum, there have been some challenges along the way. Following are three applications of our lessons learned.

You Can't Manage What You Can't Measure

Data can be likened to Lego. Much like building a Lego set, forming pieces of data into knowledge takes direction and patience. The Environmental Impact and Sustainability team receives facility, information technology, human resources, sourcing, and vendor data. We then consolidate the data into standardized formats to track progress toward environmental sustainability goals. The "crawl, walk, run" strategy for data is depicted in Exhibit 5. We leverage our existing tools (crawl) as we strive toward data-driven solutions to decarbonize the built environment in a cost-effective way (walk). Ultimately, we can deliver data-driven climate transformation programs that address investor, governmental, and consumer pressure; position the Ascension brand as climate forward; and mitigate risks to ongoing operations with resiliency plans for increased events related to climate change (run).

Previously, energy efficiency data were available only in hindsight. Now, each of our hospitals has an operations data dashboard for reporting real-time results. The Medxcel team monitors data at each hospital to ensure that Ascension facilities' operations remain compliant with policies and regulations, comfortable for patients and staff, and cost-effective for the organization. Team members can monitor data from anywhere across Ascension, and local facility leaders can access real-time information so that they know where to focus attention.

Start Small

Ascension's sustainability journey began with energy savings efforts, and that success yielded a serendipitous outcome. As hospitals

Exhibit 5: The Decarbonization Crawl, Walk, Run Approach

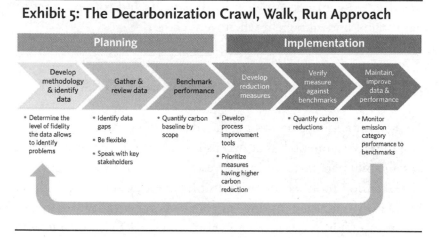

Source: Ascension. Copyright 2021 Ascension, St. Louis, Missouri. All permission requests for this image should be made to the copyright holder.

became aware of the value of improved energy efficiency, they began to ask about other sustainability strategies such as recycling programs, safer chemicals, and environmentally preferred purchasing—vividly representing the maxim "get started and the momentum will build." With environmental interests prioritized throughout the organization, associates are identifying and bringing forward more great ideas to implement systemwide.

Connect with Like-Minded Institutions

Ascension learns through its involvement with organizations dedicated to sustainability in healthcare, including Practice Greenhealth, the Health Care Without Harm Climate Council, U.S. Green Building Council, and American Hospital Association. The Catholic Health Association is another helpful resource for us. Healthcare leaders are not on this journey alone and can find ways to work together to share knowledge, resources, ideas, and solutions—the work is not proprietary. As with quality and patient safety efforts, healthcare organizations owe it to all patients and communities to get it right, and all benefit when we succeed.

ASCENSION'S IMPACT INVESTMENT STRATEGY

One may not immediately sense the connection between investment and the environment, but at Ascension, environmental impact and sustainability are factored into investment portfolio decisions.

Ascension took socially responsible investing up to a new level in 2014 when it began making "impact" investments. Impact investments can (1) improve access to goods and services for people who are vulnerable or living in poverty and (2) support environmental stewardship, such as resource conservation, green products, renewable energy, and clean water.

As Liz Foshage, CFO at Ascension, explained, "Impact investing represents an evolution of our mission-based philosophy where we don't just avoid certain investments that might violate our socially responsible investing guidelines, but we actively invest in a way that we believe will generate a social or an environmental benefit, particularly for the poor and vulnerable. This commitment attests to our interest in environmental stewardship at home and abroad" (personal communication, June 3, 2022). Since 2014, Ascension has committed a total of $128 million to 33 impact investments, including 10 specifically for environmental stewardship.

CONCLUSION

The care of God's creation is not only important to our mission, but it also is work that demands immediate attention. When we as healthcare leaders think about the future of our children, as well as the future of our organizations and the lives of our employees and patients, it becomes clear that the work toward sustainability cannot wait. Wildfires, floods, hurricanes, and extreme heat will increasingly affect the health of our communities—a tragic reality further compounded by social determinants that disproportionately cause harm to those who are least able to overcome it. As dedicated stewards and advocates for the environment, we can make a tangible difference in the lives of generations to come.

REFERENCE

Hogan, N. C. 2022. *Leading on Climate Change: How Healthcare Leaders Stop Global Warming*. Goodreads.

MY PERSONAL "WHY" FOR THIS WORK

One of the most impactful moments early in my career took place while serving at another health system in the aftermath of hurricanes Katrina and Rita. I will forever remember sitting at the transfer center in Houston around midnight, watching helicopters, fixed-wing aircraft, and ambulances set out for New Orleans to help evacuate people.

In the days to come, people arrived at the Houston Astrodome and the convention center, where we were providing care. They came with nothing other than what they could carry—totally displaced from family members and dropped off in an unfamiliar city.

I was struck by how, when the fabric of a community breaks down following a natural disaster, normal infrastructure and processes are displaced. Security, safety, food, access, and relationships get stripped away. The storms left both New Orleans and Houston forever changed. All because of a natural disaster, likely exacerbated by climate change.

As I reflect on Katrina and Rita, and the countless wildfires, floods, and extreme heat events that have happened since, I see the immediate and lasting impact these environmental events have on individuals and communities, especially for those people who are poor and vulnerable. Perhaps more urgently, I also recognize the role that I play—along with all healthcare leaders—to address the growing impact on our patients and communities.

Craig Cordola

FOR DISCUSSION

1. How is the commitment to environmental sustainability both an expectation and an opportunity to approach healthcare differently?
2. Develop a brief purpose statement, tied to your mission and values, to guide a commitment to sustainable environmental practices.
3. How can a "circular economy" reduce waste?
4. Under a change management framework, how can improved energy efficiency galvanize sustainability efforts?

Sound Environmental Practices in Healthcare Facilities Management

JONATHAN J. FLANNERY, FASHE, CHFM,
MHSA, FACHE

SUMMARY

The time has come for healthcare organizations to improve their efforts regarding their impact on the environment, particularly on the communities they serve. For years, healthcare has been at the forefront of addressing social needs with public health initiatives but has lagged on environmental concerns. By carefully reviewing their energy usage and aging infrastructures, healthcare leaders and their facility managers can do a better job of controlling healthcare's environmental impact. Green practices are key indicators of an organization's ethically focused sustainability efforts. So, while healthcare has traditionally focused on its social impact—providing healthcare services is, after all, inherently social—it must expand its community engagement by considering the environmental impact of hospitals and health systems on their communities in the context of climate change.

OVER THE PAST few years, forward-looking healthcare organizations have begun to see their role outside their walls. They are establishing measurable, strategic priorities aimed at sustainability to reduce their environmental impact and thus protect the health of those they serve.

For example, many are increasing their efforts to involve their communities in emergency responses to natural disasters. These climate-related disasters pose extremely disruptive challenges for healthcare. As anchor institutions whose facilities provide essential services for both short-term emergencies (e.g., after a storm) and long-term public health efforts (e.g., childhood obesity programs), they have expanding roles to play in their communities, regions, and beyond.

According to the Centers for Disease Control and Prevention (n.d.):

> In the U.S., public health can be affected by disruptions of physical, biological, and ecological systems, including disturbances originating [within the United States] and elsewhere. The health effects of these disruptions include increased respiratory and cardiovascular disease, injuries and premature deaths related to extreme weather events, changes in the prevalence and geographical distribution of food- and water-borne illnesses and other infectious diseases, and threats to mental health.

The Centers for Disease Control and Prevention has produced a diagram detailing several areas of impact (Exhibit 1).

As an example, hospitals and public health programs in coastal communities are taking an all-hazards approach in the face of a widening variety of potential climate-related challenges. These programs must consider short-term disruptions such as unseasonable temperature extremes and the delivery of essential health services following these events when needs are greatest. In addition, these healthcare organizations must work with their communities to

Exhibit 1: Impact of Climate Change on Human Health

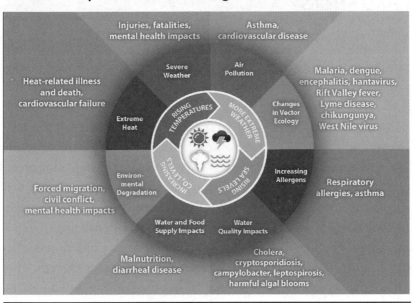

Source: Centers for Disease Control and Prevention.

address long-term disruptions such as rising sea levels. Proactive approaches now will help avoid public health shocks in the future.

According to the Office of Climate Change and Health Equity (OCCHE n.d.) of the Department of Health and Human Services, "Climate change is already increasing the severity or frequency of health threats occurring in some areas. In other areas, climate change effects on land, water, and air quality can cause new health problems where they hadn't previously occurred."

The OCCHE specifies seven areas of concern: heat, seasonal changes, air quality, temperature changes, flooding, severe weather, and healthcare system effects. Notably, "extreme climate events can place added stress on hospital and public health systems and limit people's ability to obtain adequate healthcare during crises" (OCCHE n.d.).

RESPONDING TO ENVIRONMENTAL CHALLENGES

The American Society for Health Care Engineering (ASHE), a professional membership group of the American Hospital Association for which I serve as senior associate director for advocacy, has been encouraging engagement in environmental efforts for several years through its Energy to Care program. This complimentary energy reduction program helps healthcare facilities track, manage, and communicate savings. Through benchmarking, education, and energy-saving practices, participants in the program have been able to put more than $550 million in savings back into patient care since 2010. (ASHE has received the Energy Star Partner of the Year Sustained Excellence Award in recognition of its contributions to the Environmental Protection Agency's Energy Star program. This is the fourth year in a row that ASHE has received this award, making a total of six successive years that ASHE has received an EPA ENERGY STAR Partner of the Year Award.)

One of ASHE's focal points in the environmental arena is the need to decarbonize healthcare, which is a significant contributor to global greenhouse gas emissions. According to the Health Care Climate Footprint produced by Health Care Without Harm, the sector contributes 4.4 percent of the world's net greenhouse gas emissions, totaling 2 gigatons of carbon dioxide equivalent (CO_2e) emissions (Karliner et al. 2019). In the United States, healthcare accounts for 25 percent of global emissions, the largest proportion of any country (Dzau et al. 2021).

While ASHE and its members are moving environmental efforts forward, much more work must be done to address complicating factors. For example, some current codes and standards require healthcare facilities to operate in ways that conflict with their efforts to mitigate the effects of climate change, such as regular testing of emergency generators.

ADDRESSING AGING INFRASTRUCTURE

To some degree, the current state of healthcare infrastructure is confounding environmental efforts. Research conducted by capital planning firm Facility Health and commissioned by ASHE shows that the average percentage of deferred maintenance across US healthcare facilities is 41 percent; the outlay needed to address that deferred maintenance today is projected to exceed $243 billion (Morgan 2021).

Within the healthcare engineering context, the core infrastructure consists of the following:

- life safety components such as fire alarms, automatic transfer switches, and fire pumps;
- heating, ventilation, and air conditioning (HVAC), plumbing, and major mechanical components such as air handlers and conditioners, boilers, compressors, cooling towers, and domestic hot water systems;
- electrical components such as primary and emergency distribution systems;
- building integrity, access, and mobility components such as windows, security systems, elevators, and helipads;
- critical support components such as medical gas inventory/ distribution systems, climate control systems, and electronic health record systems; and
- additional major components such as clinical engineering assets (direct patient care), civil engineering assets (grounds, parking garages), branding assets (signage), and FFE (i.e., furniture, fixtures, equipment).

When these assets have exceeded industry-expected useful life based on age and/or condition but remain serviceable, deferred maintenance may become an issue. Infrastructure currently in deferred maintenance status does not mean that the assets are in imminent failure mode. However, that status signals an increased probability of failure and therefore risk to patients. If the rate of deferred maintenance continues to increase at its current rate ($12 billion to $18 billion per year), the amount needed to address that deferred maintenance will increase to $391 billion over 10 years (Morgan 2021). The aging infrastructure of the nation's healthcare system is an inescapable fact that must be addressed.

While facing climate-related disasters amid the current state of deferred maintenance in healthcare, US hospitals and health systems also have been caring for patients with COVID-19, comforting families, and protecting communities nonstop since the onset of the pandemic in early 2020. The pandemic has strained hospitals' and health systems' finances with dramatic negative effects on operating margins. Exacerbating this problem are Medicare sequestration cuts along with payment increases that are well below increases in costs. An analysis by Premier Inc. found that for the fiscal year 2022, hospitals received a 2.4 percent increase in their Medicare inpatient payment rate, while hospital labor rates increased 6.5 percent (American Hospital Association 2022). These numbers reflect a direct impact on healthcare organizations' ability to address their aging infrastructure.

Climate-related disasters will continue to increase in intensity and frequency, and the direct force of these events along with the aforementioned financial impact on healthcare organizations will impair their ability to maintain the infrastructure of their facilities. And as the infrastructure continues to age and be placed in deferred maintenance status, healthcare organizations will have a more difficult time responding to climate-related disasters. This spiraling effect will compromise the resiliency of healthcare organizations, thus increasing risk to patients and jeopardizing the ability of these organizations to provide essential services.

As ASHE concludes:

> The infrastructure of U.S. health care is not in critical condition, but it is aging. As with anything that ages, it

takes more resources to keep existing facilities in top working order. Some professionally recognized and validated indicators show that investment in these resources has declined. Thus, early and responsible financial investment in our healthcare infrastructure can mitigate this trend, enhance safety, and improve performance, which will eventually allow us to allocate more resources to direct patient care. In addition, now more than ever, healthcare organizations need competent, motivated professionals to maintain and operate healthcare facilities. These professionals must have the right mix of determination, ingenuity, skills, and competencies to ensure that legacy facilities are capable of providing the same positive patient outcomes that a new state-of-the-art facility can provide. (King et al. 2017)

APPLYING SOUND CAPITAL PLANNING PRACTICES

Even as they face the challenges noted here, healthcare organizations can limit their environmental footprint. Steps can be taken to improve facility infrastructure and reduce deferred maintenance through careful capital planning while advancing operational efforts to reduce greenhouse gas emissions and energy use. Recommended steps for capital planning by facilities managers follow.

- **Step 1.** Validate current performance. Conduct a facility condition assessment, validate asset inventory, and understand current asset performance.
- **Step 2.** Construct an initial capital plan. Applying the data from Step 1, develop a data-driven capital plan.
- **Step 3.** Optimize data integrity and maintenance. Continuously update asset condition and risk scores over time, modify asset useful life, and model capital planning.

Optimize capital investments based on asset risk and performance.

- **Step 4.** Monitor continuous improvement and risk mitigation. Determine the results of investments, quantify those results through improving index scores, optimize ongoing maintenance strategies, and avoid emergent repairs. Follow the data and then celebrate success.
- **Step 5.** Document reduced environmental impact. Record reductions in environmental impact through all efforts of the organization. This will help build the framework of the organization's environmental, social, and governance efforts within the environmental focus.

Recommended steps to improve operational environmental efforts follow.

- **Step 1.** Join and actively participate in ASHE's Energy to Care program. By tracking, managing, and communicating energy savings, healthcare facility managers can accurately adjust the energy used to continuously operate a facility.
- **Step 2.** Understand nondiscretionary spending. Mandatory facility workload can be broken down into two general categories:
  - *Compliance-driven workload:* The cost of those activities required to meet regulatory compliance codes and standards.
  - *Asset-driven workload:* The cost to operate and perform break/fix services to meet the demands of the daily operations of the facility.
- **Step 3.** Understand the total cost to perform preventive maintenance, which comprises the costs of those activities to staff and fund a preventive maintenance program.

CONCLUSION

By taking the facility planning and operational steps listed here—adjusting as appropriate to the organization's mission and values—healthcare leaders and their facility managers can move their environmental efforts forward and effectively manage an organization's E challenges within the ESG framework. Rewards can be achieved by managing energy usage and thus reducing greenhouse gas emissions. And by improving infrastructure through carefully planned and executed capital improvements, an organization can move beyond maintenance mode and truly manage its environmental impact.

REFERENCES

American Hospital Association. 2022. "Massive Growth in Expenses and Rising Inflation Fuel Continued Financial Challenges for America's Hospitals and Health Systems." Cost of Caring Report. Published April 2022. www.aha.org/costsofcaring.

Centers for Disease Control and Prevention. n.d. "Climate Effects on Health." Accessed June 13, 2021. www.cdc.gov/climateandhealth/effects/default.htm.

Dzau, V. J., R. Levine, G. Barrett, and A. Witty. 2021. "Decarbonizing the U.S. Health Sector—A Call to Action." *New England Journal of Medicine* 385: 2117–9. https://doi.org/10.1056/NEJMp2115675.

Karliner, J., S. Slotterback, R. Boyd, B. Ashby, and K. Steele. 2019. "Health Care's Climate Footprint: How the Health Sector Contributes to the Global Climate Crisis, and Opportunities for Action." Health Care Without Harm, Climatesmart health care series, Green Paper Number One. Produced in collaboration with Arup. Published September 2019. https://noharmglobal.org/sites/default/files/documents-files/5961/HealthCaresClimateFootprint_092319.pdf.

King, D., C. Beebe, J. Suchomel, P. Bardwell, V. Della Donna, and L. Walt. 2017. "State of U.S. Health Care Facility Infrastructure." American Society for Health Care Engineering Monograph. https://www.ashe.org/facilityinfrastructure.

Morgan, J. 2021. "AHA Advocates for Investments in Aging Health Care Infrastructure." *Health Facilities Management.* Published June 30, 2021. https://www.hfmmagazine.com /articles/4212aha-advocates-for-investments-in-aging-health care-infrastructure.

Office of Climate Change and Health Equity (OCCHE). n.d. "Climate Change and Health Equity." Accessed June 13, 2022. https://www .hhs.gov/climate-change-health-equity-environmentaljustice /climate-change-health-equity/index.html.

FOR DISCUSSION

1. Regarding the structural integrity of their facilities, what are some short-term climate disruptions that healthcare organizations must face? What are some long-term disruptions?

2. How is the current state of healthcare infrastructure confounding environmental initiatives?

3. How can your capital planning process be improved to consider financial challenges and other complications as described?

The Impact of Environmental Factors on Credit Ratings in Healthcare

EMILY E. WADHWANI, FACHE

SUMMARY

At their core, credit ratings are holistic assessments of relative credit risk, inclusive of both quantitative and qualitative factors. Environmental, social, and governance (ESG) considerations have always been implicitly incorporated in credit rating methodology as components of a hospital or health system's wider performance. More recently, however, ESG effects have been explicitly identified. While social and governance considerations are important to credit ratings, the impact of environmental factors on rating outcomes in the healthcare sector continues to expand exponentially. This movement reflects the varied ways in which climate change, resource and materials management, energy management, and water management can affect credit profiles. The shift to a lower carbon-dependent economy also presents opportunities for issuers that make meaningful transitions toward renewable energy sources.

As Exhibits 1 and 2 illustrate, environmental, social, and governance (ESG) considerations have long been implicitly incorporated in credit rating methodology as components of a hospital or health system's performance. Since 2019, the impact of ESG has been more transparently signaled through Fitch's ESG Relevance Scores, which assign values to the significance and materiality of ESG factors for a rating decision.

What are the "E"—environmental—issues facing the healthcare sector (particularly acute care providers), and what are their implications for credit rating outcomes? For this analysis, Fitch considers several areas such as climate change, resource and materials management, energy management, and water management. The impact of each area on ratings can become evident in profitability and cash flow disruptions, regulatory and litigation issues, and reputational risks.

And although it is a different ESG factor, governance and its direct role in the execution of sustainability-related policy is intertwined with long-term credit performance.

Many assets (e.g., inpatient bed towers) that are being planned or built today can be expected to be in use into the 2040s and

Exhibit 1: ESG Relevance to USPF Issuers, by Category

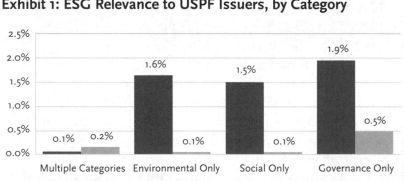

Source: FitchRatings.

Note: Data as of May 11, 2023. This chart shows categories that are driving the highest credit impact for issuers. ESG = environmental, social, and governance; USPF = US Public Finance at Fitch.

Exhibit 2: ESG Relevance to USPF Healthcare Portfolio, by Category

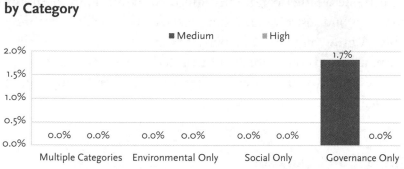

■ Medium　　■ High

Source: FitchRatings.

Note: Data as of May 11, 2023. This chart shows categories that are driving the highest credit impact for healthcare issuers. ESG = environmental, social, and governance; USPF = US Public Finance at Fitch.

2050s—even beyond, in the case of infrastructure. This timeframe coincides with when many physical climate risks of particular concern are projected to reach their extremes (Intergovernmental Panel on Climate Change 2022). Healthcare leaders should therefore mix mitigation strategies into their strategic capital planning efforts now by identifying ways to enhance the resiliency of their physical assets as well as the plausible risks associated with the entire infrastructure.

CLIMATE CHANGE

Impact on Physical Assets

Exposure to environmental forces raises alarm in the healthcare sector, given its reliance on costly and sophisticated physical plants. Some construction project costs can exceed $4 million per inpatient bed, such that a fairly small 250-bed hospital can cost as much as $1 billion to construct, equip, and open on time. These concerns can materialize in substantial rebuilding costs after natural disasters or extreme weather conditions, followed by insurance premiums increases and lost revenue from periods when facilities are unusable. A growing worry for many organizations is the impact of natural hazards on uninsured or underinsured assets and inventory, especially with greater weather extremes seen throughout the United States.

Impact on Operations

Exposure to extreme weather and physical climate risks can be either acute or chronic for a hospital or healthcare system. Physical climate risks include passing events such as hurricanes, floods, and fires; the risks can also relate to persistent longer-term changes in weather patterns and climate variability that trigger changes in rainfall, sea levels, and temperatures. To date, most adaptations have addressed acute events, oftentimes as responses to repeated or especially severe events. An example of this approach is the complete rebuilding of the Veterans Administration Medical Center and Charity Hospital in New Orleans, Louisiana, after Hurricane Katrina. Rather than make repairs, the administration decided to build a new, more durable teaching hospital in an adjacent neighborhood.

Moving forward, better and more accessible climate risk data and targeted analyses will provide a refined context that can help healthcare administrative and operational leaders do a better job of evaluating their exposure to the chronic physical effects of climate change—effects that may result in escalating insurance premiums or the withdrawal of insurers from a market, as well as increases in capital expenditures to enhance infrastructure resilience.

In the face of both ongoing and likely environmental events, management preparedness in planning, asset management and risk mitigation—and financial flexibility—are increasingly important, as Fitch's rating considerations will continue to focus on them.

MATERIALS MANAGEMENT

Expanding urbanization and growing personal income inevitably increase the demand for new construction, which can contribute to more waste and damaged ecosystems. Data from the United Nations (2018) shown in Exhibit 3 point to a continued shift in populations living in urban versus rural areas. If this trend continues as expected (despite potential lower urbanization rates in the immediate wake of the COVID-19 pandemic), the sprawl will directly diminish surrounding green spaces and farming land and compromise local ecosystems. As they follow their service markets, healthcare facilities must play an important role in the responsible stewardship of their surrounding environments, particularly given the capital-intensive nature of hospital operations.

Many hospitals are seeking certifications such as Leadership in Energy and Environmental Design (LEED) from the US Green Building Council. While construction standards vary by state and locale, LEED certification is a nationally recognized indication of energy efficiency, adaptation to climate change, water use, land use, and biodiversity preservation. The establishment of some of these goals has no direct impact on operating performance, and thus credit

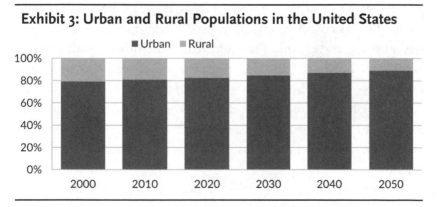

Exhibit 3: Urban and Rural Populations in the United States

Source: FitchRatings and United Nations Department of Economic and Social Affairs, Population Division (2018).

ratings. It is important to note, however, that issuers can expect lower operating and capital costs with LEED buildings because of their improved structural durability and the environmental hazard mitigation planning to address physical climate events.

ENERGY MANAGEMENT

Energy management can be critical to hospital operations because it heavily influences operational disruption and overall expenses. Nonetheless, energy and fuel use patterns are often shaped by factors outside of a hospital or health system's direct control, particularly where it is dependent on a local grid for energy. Regulated utilities, pipelines, and networks have borne the bulk of additional costs from renewable energy integration in recent years, but they eventually pass most of these costs on to end users.

To aid efficiency, carbon-related considerations continue to inform energy management decisions across the healthcare sector. Drawing upon the UN Principles for Responsible Investment's Inevitable Policy Response scenarios posted at www.unpri.org, which include a plausible policy scenario of rapid low-carbon transition from the mid-2020s, Fitch expects public policy as well as public sentiment to drive the transition away from carbon-intensive assets such as coal-fired energy plants. Certain sectors such as oil, gas, utilities, and chemical manufacturing are more exposed to this transition, but in the absence of mitigation efforts, this transition could have a wide impact on credit ratings in the long term. On one side of the equation sits the required capital or operational expenditure to improve emissions performance, and on the other side are the litigation or reputational risks associated with emissions and air-quality issues.

Even as healthcare's use of the green bond market (which supports sustainability endeavors) is increasing, the activity remains limited. These fresh endeavors seek to improve energy efficiency and bolster renewable deployment (e.g., with off-grid systems) both internally and across the supply chain. Although they have not yet ushered in a strategic sea change in hospital campus energy platforms, Fitch anticipates an escalating push for more sustainable energy plants, eventually moving facilities to a fully renewable energy platform as both consumer and legislative intentions gain momentum.

WATER MANAGEMENT

Healthcare providers use a great deal of water for essential purposes that include cleaning and sanitation, the functioning and sterilization of medical equipment, and treating wastewater for pharmaceutical residue.

When communities experience water supply constraints, the negative impact on their economies can have a trickle-down effect on local funding capacity for public health and related public finance budgets. With prolonged or repeated droughts, affected regions can suffer economic decline—particularly if economic growth plans and even livability become untenable. Thus, an acute issue can evolve into a chronic credit concern in a healthcare market over time. In California, for example, water usage restrictions in response to historic drought conditions have increased the importance of resource management, water conservation, and drought preparation and planning. Drought conditions also have exacerbated wildfire hazards with increasing frequency—an additional risk that can result in major disruptions to hospital operations and prompt rating pressure.

INCREASING INVESTOR INTEREST

Sustainable Investing

According to BloombergNEF, global sustainable debt issuance surpassed $1.6 trillion in 2021, more than double the debt issued in 2020 (Henze 2022; Rutigliano 2022). More than $51 billion of that issuance flowed into sustainable funds in the United States (Henze 2022; Rutigliano 2022). Municipal investors have been increasingly transparent about ESG's growing importance in their buying decisions, and many have established "impact funds" to support those sustainability goals.

Thus far, issuance within not-for-profit healthcare has been limited to green bond transactions (from self-designated to externally verified), with much of the issuance project-based. One hurdle for issuers is the lack of identifiable price differential in green bonds versus traditional bonds (i.e., green bonds have no significant price advantage). Also, investors are demanding more standardized disclosure around ESG—another possible barrier. As disclosure increases in quantity and comparability, investor interest and a favorable pricing differential in bond transactions likely will increase too.

Disclosure Matters

As with other reporting requirements, the emphasis on transparent and consistent disclosure regarding ESG impact will make it more important to understand how ESG factors affect healthcare providers. A proposal by the US Securities and Exchange Commission (SEC 2021) focuses on the financial materiality of corporations' physical risks and opportunities, as well as the transition risks in a shift to a low-carbon economy. In its proposal, the SEC calls for both qualitative and quantitative information.

The proposal does not apply to not-for-profit healthcare providers because they are not registered with the SEC. Nevertheless, the sector remains exposed to physical climate risks as well as climate transition risks. Fitch therefore expects that US Public Finance at Fitch issuers will face greater demand for ESG disclosure from investors, particularly on climate risks. The SEC's municipal securities rulemaking board expressed its interest in these matters through a request for information for public input on ESG practices in the municipal securities market. The request covered ESG-related risk factors, including a question about whether any of those factors could pose a systemic risk to the municipal securities market. There was a general consensus among commenters that "ESG practices in the municipal securities market are still evolving. Many commenters noted that market-based solutions are still emerging and, as a result, premature regulatory action could inhibit further development of best practices" (Municipal Securities Rulemaking Board 2022, p. 9).

US bank regulators are also developing frameworks that would measure banks' longer-term risks related to climate change, which could affect their capital investment programs. The Federal Reserve Bank, the US Financial Stability Oversight Council, the Office of the Comptroller of the Currency, and the Federal Deposit Insurance Corporation have all issued preliminary guidance on paths to assess and mitigate the financial risks associated with climate change. The fallout from prospective requirements to bolster bank capitalization rates may lead to reduced investment in higher-emissions industries or geographical regions exposed to the physical impacts of climate change. Either path could challenge service area economic stability and healthcare provider expansion plans, thus potentially affecting issuer credit quality.

THE IMPACT ON RATINGS

Operational and Cash Flow Risks

Changes in energy-efficiency standards, grid energy costs, or disruption to energy supply can affect revenue trends, increase operating costs, and add capital spending needs through the requirement for new infrastructure and alternative logistics arrangements.

One painful example of disruption was the failure of the Texas power grid during severe winter weather in February 2021. Many hospitals across the state faced difficulties related to the weather besides blackouts, including water service stoppages, reduced food deliveries, and the inability of staff to get to work. State and federal funds may have ultimately mitigated the financial impact, but the near-term harm to hospital activities was severe.

Regulatory and Litigation Risk

Regulatory compliance costs have increased in the past decade as a result of tightening air emission standards overseen by multiple regulators with overlapping remits.

The Biden administration has outlined a clear commitment to reducing carbon emissions and has established the Office of Climate Change and Health Equity within the US Department of Health and Human Services to make the case for reducing the carbon footprint in healthcare and establishing best practices for doing so. While financial incentives or penalties have yet to be incorporated, the long view is that this will be an area of expanded regulation and reporting.

Reputational Risks

Hospitals and health systems are appropriately mindful of patient and public perceptions as they manage their brands. These perceptions can shift rapidly in response to changing social agendas and policies; negative perceptions can have an irrevocable impact on the competitive landscape in a crowded market.

Governance and Management

While not an explicit component of an environmental analysis under an ESG framework, governance factors guide the institutional response to environmental issues, so they are highly relevant to ratings. As illustrated in Exhibit 2, governance continues to be the single most important ESG factor in healthcare, as it directly affects the quality of service. Successful implementation of governance policies, without undue interference from appointed boards or elected officials, remains crucial to strong financial and operating performance. (The third section of this book closely examines the role of governance in healthcare ESG initiatives.)

CONCLUSION

ESG considerations have always been incorporated in credit rating methodology as components of a hospital or health system's performance. Recently, however, the effects have been more explicitly identified. As an important part of that trend, the role of environmental factors continues to grow, reflecting the varied ways in which climate change, resource and materials management, energy management, and water management can affect credit profiles.

ACKNOWLEDGMENTS

The author thanks Fitch colleagues Kevin Holloran, senior director and sector lead of NFP Healthcare, and Marcy Block, senior director of ESG Analytics, Global Public Finance and Infrastructure, for their contributions.

REFERENCES

Henze, V. 2022. "Sustainable Debt Issuance Breezed Past $1.6 Trillion in 2021." Bloomberg NEF. Published January 12. https://about.bnef.com/blog/sustainable-debt-issuance-breezed-past-1-6-trillion-in-2021/.

Intergovernmental Panel on Climate Change. 2022. "Climate Change 2022: Impacts, Adaptation and Vulnerability." https://www.ipcc.ch/report/ar6/wg2/downloads/report/IPCC_AR6_WGII_SummaryForPolicymakers.pdf.

Municipal Securities Rulemaking Board. 2022. "Summary of Responses to the MSRB's Request for Information on ESG Practices in the Municipal Securities Market." Published August. www.msrb.org/sites/default/files/2022-09/Summary -of-Responses-to-MSRB-ESG-RFI-August-2022.pdf.

Rutigliano, M. 2022. "1H 2022 Sustainable Finance Market Outlook." BloombergNEF. Published January 24. https:// about.bnef.com/blog/1h-2022-sustainable-finance-market -outlook/#:~:text=In%202021%2C%20more%20than%20 %241.6,market%20to%20over%20%244%20trillion.

Securities and Exchange Commission (SEC). 2021. "SEC Announces Enforcement Task Force Focused on Climate and ESG Issues." Published March 4. https://www.sec.gov/news/ press-release/2021-42.

United Nations Department of Economic and Social Affairs, Population Division. 2018. "2018 Revision of World Urbanization Prospects." Published May 16. www.un.org/development/desa /publications/2018-revision-of-worldurbanization-prospects .html.

FOR DISCUSSION

1. The impact of ESG is signaled through Fitch's ESG Relevance Scores. What do those scores consider?
2. Healthcare's use of the green bond market is increasing, although the activity remains limited. How could this market serve the interests of your healthcare facilities?
3. As ESG considerations become more explicitly incorporated in credit rating methodology, to what extent will business practices affect credit profiles, and therefore credit availability?

Social Issues

An Effective Response to Healthcare Disparities Begins with a Strategic Plan

DENISE BROOKS-WILLIAMS, FACHE

SUMMARY

For too long, healthcare disparities have negatively affected underrepresented groups in urban areas throughout the United States. Disparities in care and outcomes related to social determinants were known, and efforts were made to address them. Effective change for all moved up to top priority in the wake of COVID-19's arrival, police brutality, social unrest, and the murders of Black Americans, including George Floyd. Henry Ford Health (HFH), working with leading local community organizations, immediately pledged to address social and racial injustices. Unfortunately, many neighborhoods still suffer disproportionately from maternal and infant mortality, food insecurity, and other social vulnerabilities. HFH's commitment to equity includes creatively meeting the needs of the underserved. HFH has developed innovative ways to address the social, economic, and educational challenges to the health of Metro Detroit. Through thoughtful consideration and passionate leadership, HFH is strategically creating authentic and scalable social change to address racism and discrimination in healthcare.

Over the years, healthcare in the United States has made incredible strides forward, and yet diverse and underrepresented communities do not always experience improved care and outcomes. Underrepresented populations disproportionately suffer from cancer, cardiovascular diseases, depression, and pregnancy-related complications. In a land of justice for all, profound racial and ethnic health disparities persist.

Detroit sees some of the most significant disparities in the United States. According to the 2020 US Census, the population of Michigan's largest city was 639,111, with more than 77 percent identifying as Black or African American. Headquartered in the heart of the city, Henry Ford Health (HFH) serves Detroit and surrounding communities. Addressing healthcare disparities and social determinants of health (SDOHs) is a part of the foundation of HFH's mission. This commitment was magnified following the confirmed arrival of COVID-19 in 2020 and the fallout from the murders of Black Americans, including George Floyd in 2020. HFH has taken strong actions to address social and racial injustices, starting with a deeper dive into health disparities and other barriers to equitable care.

Days after Floyd's murder, HFH President and CEO Wright Lassiter III (now CEO of CommonSpirit) announced the creation of the On the Journey to Equity for All initiative, HFH's diversity, equity, inclusion, and social justice (DEIJ) strategic plan. While our system had been recognized nationwide for its efforts for years, the DEIJ strategic plan formalized our continuing commitments to antiracism and social justice advocacy, a diverse workforce and inclusive culture, community empowerment, and healthcare equity.

Of course, we knew we had to do more than simply put together a plan. We also needed a way to hold ourselves accountable and make a real impact in our community. This is why we decided to track our progress toward milestones to gauge the significance of the completed metrics toward our DEIJ commitments by 2025. A major part of this strategy is our work with the community with the adoption of measures of success to track progress. Our partners include the Community Health and Social Services (CHASS) Clinic (a federally qualified health center) and Generation with Promise (a nonprofit that helps children lead healthy change in their homes and communities), along with our local nutrition outreach and programs in which nurses work with local parishes to provide health information to their congregation. To understand why this work is crucial, it is important to define what it means and for whom it is working.

THE PURSUIT OF HEALTHCARE EQUITY

If health equity is achieved only when every person has the same access to care, regardless of background, gender, ethnicity, or socioeconomic status, then the sad reality is that the United States—with its vast wealth and medical abilities—has fallen short. According to the Commonwealth Fund (Schneider et al. 2021), the US health system trails 10 other high-income countries in affordability, administrative efficiency, equity, and outcomes of care. The same study suggests that half of lower-income US adults reported that costs prevented them from getting needed healthcare, compared to 27 percent of higher-income adults. (In the United Kingdom, only 12 percent of people with lower incomes and 7 percent with higher incomes reported financial barriers to care.)

How do we in the healthcare sector lead improvement in these numbers? To start, the task can be as simple as focusing on communication. For example, it is a harrowing reality that Black women (along with American Indian and Alaska Native women) are three times more likely to die from a pregnancy-related cause than white women (Petersen et al. 2019). Why? The reason could be chronic conditions or the quality of healthcare—or it could be they were not listened to when they tried to access care. As a widely publicized example, tennis star Serena Williams suffered a serious postpartum complication and later contended that she had to fiercely advocate for herself to prevent a serious or fatal outcome from an undetected blood clot. Her experience is a clear illustration of what countless non-white women go through every single day. HFH has worked to address this issue through structured virtual training of staff to mitigate communication barriers in our labor and delivery units. The new training is being implemented across campuses throughout the system.

HFH leadership is proud of this new training, but we want to do more. As part of the DEIJ strategic plan, we are aiming for the root cause of maternal mortality through mandatory implicit bias training and trauma-informed care training. The goal is to reduce the rates of severe maternal postpartum hemorrhage in Black and Hispanic women by 40 percent by 2025. HFH is also prioritizing efforts to reduce the risk of sudden unexplained infant death syndrome, which disproportionately affects non-white babies (Mayo Clinic n.d.).

To reach our goals, we need talented, diverse individuals. HFH is aiming to be a magnet for health equity researchers nationally by creating a postdoctoral training program to accommodate four underrepresented minority researchers concentrating on health disparities. Diversity is critical in medical research because different diseases and conditions do not affect everyone the same way. A lack of diversity in clinical trials can lead to outcomes that only work for certain groups.

A HEALTHY COMMUNITY'S NEEDS GO BEYOND MEDICINE

To improve the health of their communities, health systems must implement more public and internal education programs that fight racial bias and health disparities. A healthy community is represented by more than just the medical status of the population. The path to equity covers the whole person as an individual and the social vulnerabilities they might face that lead to health disparities and poor health conditions.

Social vulnerabilities in a community are related to the availability of vital resources such as clean water and air, access to nutritious food at a fair cost, support from loved ones, and a stable living environment. Frequently, these vulnerabilities are linked to health, but the ties may not be obvious at first. For example, we had a patient repeatedly coming into an emergency department with respiratory issues. Our well-trained doctors and nurses did the right examinations, but not until the third visit did the patient mention their difficulty with breathing in the hot weather. By engaging in additional discussion, staff learned that the patient had no air conditioning at home. HFH provided an air conditioner, thus creating a healthier environment.

Social barriers to healthy lives were highlighted during the height of the COVID-19 pandemic. In Detroit, at a time when Black people represented more than 75 percent of known COVID-19 diagnoses and nearly 90 percent of deaths, they were also more likely to be very concerned about being evicted and needing rent assistance (Ray et al. 2021). HFH, through a grant, provided a hotel room post-discharge for COVID-19 patients who were housing insecure. We also collaborated with food banks in response to related food insecurity. Although healthcare organizations cannot address all SDOHs and fix all social problems, our DEIJ strategy illustrates an effective way to understand unhealthy conditions that exist and then actively communicate with people to address those conditions.

COMMUNITY EMPOWERMENT

Ultimately, we at HFH want more than just a healthy community. We need a community that is empowered to thrive, and empowering a community means supporting equity. By listening to patients and disadvantaged people and identifying social barriers to care, health systems can take action to create and sustain health in historically marginalized communities.

In applying our DEIJ strategic plan to meet these challenges to a healthy community, we have increased Tier 1 diverse local supplier spending and pledged $15 million of investable long-term operating cash-based assets to foster community wealth building. We are also reducing social needs barriers to high-quality healthcare using a community information exchange platform. Through this shared technology platform to coordinate services and collect data, we aim to close 50 percent of identified social needs gaps by 2025.

RECRUITMENT AND DIVERSIFYING THE PIPELINE

To best serve the particular needs of a disadvantaged community, healthcare professionals should reflect the diverse makeup of the community they serve. Diversity includes race, socioeconomic background, sexual orientation, gender, religion, and ethnicity. Unfortunately, the United States suffers from gaps in representation in healthcare. According to the Association of American Medical Colleges (2019), only about 5 percent of physicians identify as Black/African American, despite this group making up 13 percent of the US population. Fewer than 6 percent of physicians identify as Hispanic, despite Hispanics making up 19 percent of the US population. When patients are treated by someone they can relate to and can communicate with clearly and honestly, they can enjoy an enhanced opportunity to achieve better health. HFH supports this opportunity with a leadership commitment to diversity. Leaders serve as cross-cultural mentors—executive sponsors—to individuals from a race/ethnicity/gender different from their own. A diverse leadership team ensures a range of ideas and perspectives in decision-making, thus creating a more positive working environment that we believe can lead to improved talent retention and reduce health disparities. We also have a diversity council that includes various levels of leaders in the organization who work to drive DEIJ across the system.

Having a diverse and inclusive workforce requires a commitment on all levels, starting with an organization's leadership team and board. HFH is actively engaged in developing inclusive workforce practices. As part of our DEIJ strategic plan, we are increasing underrepresented minority talent in leadership and management to

at least 25 percent throughout HFH by 2025. We are also fostering
DEIJ awareness through 100 percent leader participation in quarterly
listening sessions with staff, training on inclusive leadership practices
and culture, and unconscious bias training, with new programs
implemented annually.

THE POWER OF SOCIAL ADVOCACY

A truly equitable healthcare system goes beyond the walls of a hospital or doctor's office. It is crucial for healthcare systems to actively
reject and eliminate all forms of bias, racism, and violence in their
communities.

HFH is engaged in social justice advocacy activities at national,
state, and local levels, as measured in our social justice report card.
We are "walking the talk" regarding respectful policing with implicit
bias training for all security officers. And we are advocating relent-
lessly for social justice in our communities. This advocacy includes
several goals to be achieved by 2025 such as:

- providing access to behavioral healthcare in HFH's school-
  based clinics to interrupt the school-to-prison pipeline;
- doubling the healthcare organizations in our market
  that participate in the national Ban the Box campaign
  to remove the question "Have you been convicted of a
  felony?" from most job applications; and
- achieving top ranking in a survey that evaluates HFH's
  public brand perception around DEIJ. Using this
  information, we can adjust our efforts if necessary.

Some of these goals may be very ambitious, but we also know
that improvement is nonnegotiable for our organization. Social
justice in our communities directly translates to providing high-
quality healthcare for all. Every voice is needed to create a healthy
community.

CONCLUSION

Society has a long way to go when it comes to addressing the health inequities that underserved people experience in the US healthcare system. The good news is that these issues are being addressed by HFH and many other organizations. Continued progress will be possible only if healthcare leaders include DEIJ strategies and environmental, social, and governance imperatives in their foundational work and continue to focus on the elimination of healthcare disparities in their local communities. If the challenges we have collectively faced over the past few years have taught us anything, it is that no matter our backgrounds or how we identify, we are better, healthier, and stronger when we work together and care about each other.

REFERENCES

Association of American Medical Colleges (AAMC). 2019. "Diversity in Medicine: Facts and Figures 2019." https://www.aamc .org/data-reports/workforce/ interactive-data/figure-18-percent age-all-activephysicians-race/ethnicity-2018.

Mayo Clinic. n.d. "Sudden Infant Death Syndrome (SIDS)." https:// www.mayoclinic.org/diseases-conditions/sudden-infant-death -syndrome/symptoms-causes/syc-20352800.

Petersen, E. E., N. L. Davis, D. Goodman, S. Cox, C. Syverson, K. Seed, C. Shapiro-Mendoza, W. M. Callaghan, and W. Barfield. 2019. "Racial/Ethnic Disparities in Pregnancy-Related Deaths—United States, 2007–2016." Morbidity and Mortality Weekly Report 68 (35): 762–65. https://www.cdc.gov/mmwr /volumes/68/wr/mm6835a3.htm?s_cid=mm6835a3_w.

Ray, R., J. F. Morgan, L. Wileden, S. Elizondo, and D. Wiley-Yancy. 2021. "Examining and Addressing COVID-19 Racial Disparities in Detroit." Brookings Institution and New Detroit. https://

www.newdetroit.org/examining-and-addressing-covid-19-racial
-disparities-indetroit//.

Schneider, E. C., A. Shah, M. M. Doty, R. Tikkanen, K. Fields,
and R. D. Williams II. 2021. "Mirror, Mirror 2021: Reflecting
Poorly—Health Care in the U.S. Compared to Other High-
Income Countries." The Commonwealth Fund. https://www
.commonwealthfund.org/publications/fundreports/2021/aug
/mirror-mirror-2021-reflectingpoorly.

FOR DISCUSSION

1. Why is it important to codify a formal strategic plan that ensures commitments to diversity, equity, inclusion, and social justice?
2. How can your organization track progress in its work with its community? What should be measured?
3. Who are the potential partners that can help expand your community impact?
4. Henry Ford Hospital has instituted a cross-cultural mentorship program to support internal diversity. What is the value of that program? How can a similar program work in your organization?

Equity Rx: Boston Medical Center's Work to Accelerate Racial Health Justice

KATE WALSH

SUMMARY

In November 2021, after more than a year of investigating the racial health disparities across its organization, Boston Medical Center launched the Health Equity Accelerator, a system-wide approach to holistically address the root causes of health inequities among people of different races and ethnicities and speed improvements in health outcomes. This article discusses lessons learned during the institution's process of discovery, shares examples of the work to dismantle a structural narrative that impedes health justice, and outlines interventions that can be applied to other healthcare systems across the United States.

DAILY, DOCTORS TYPE up prescriptions and send their ailing patients to the pharmacy. But for healthcare systems serving majority Black, Hispanic, Latino/a, Indigenous, and Asian populations from disinvested communities, the cure for what ails people cannot be found at a pharmacy. Despite decades of advancements in clinical care, health inequities persist across the nation.

For us at Boston Medical Center (BMC), New England's largest safety-net hospital and the primary teaching affiliate for the Boston University School of Medicine, these disparities are deeply troubling. About two-thirds of our patient population identify with a marginalized racial or ethnic group. They are also frequently entrenched in racist systems that impede wealth creation. More than 60 percent of our patient population receives public insurance; approximately half have a household income below the federal poverty level. We see the health impact on our patients as they struggle with low-wage jobs, food deserts, and substandard housing.

BEYOND THE PILL BOTTLE

For decades, all of us at BMC have taken pride in our leading work to "think beyond the pill bottle" by instead prescribing solutions to address the upstream drivers of poor health, from nourishing food to stable housing. Since its first prescription in 2001, our Preventive Food Pantry has grown to provide healthy groceries to 7,500 patients and their families each month. And because housing instability is a driver of adverse health outcomes, we began coordinating with community partners to help medically complex families obtain housing in 2016, an initiative that has reduced rates of poor health in children (Bovell-Ammon et al. 2020).

Building on these innovations, we have continued to lead. We prioritized economic mobility by helping patients collect tax refunds and open their 529 college savings plan accounts at the doctor's office. We embarked on multi-institutional job creation and training projects that create pathways to career ladders. While these initiatives improved many lives, the horrific events that spurred America's reckoning on race in 2020, coupled with COVID-19's disproportionate devastation on the nation's communities of color, revealed that our actions were not delivering equitable care fast enough.

At the height of the pandemic in Boston, Black residents were 1.6 times more likely than white residents to die from COVID-19; Latino/a residents bore more than double the burden of infections than non-Latinos/as. Looking at health data beyond the pandemic, we found Boston's communities of color had health outcomes consistently 1.5–3 times worse than their non-Latino/a–white counterparts in Boston. Even when controlling for economic status, racial differences persist in outcomes such as pregnancy-related deaths, premature cancer mortality, and mental health (Boston Medical Center 2021). Uncovering these statistics in a city renowned for its healthcare and research institutions—at an institution with a long-standing commitment to exceptional care without exception—we realized our efforts to improve health for all patients were insufficient. Helping patients maintain their health is core to every hospital's mission, and to do that job it is essential to rethink how health systems address race.

At BMC, we believe health system leaders must hold themselves accountable, uncover the racism entrenched in societal systems and healthcare policies, and shift efforts from simply filling gaps to eliminating them. We need to be explicit about what it will take to meet the needs of the moment. Transforming healthcare in such a profound, fundamental manner requires humility to investigate and question what we think we know, focus to give this work sustained priority, and resources to fund the necessary restructuring of operations.

Emphasizing Innovation and Equity

Unfortunately, the hospitals that serve Black, Indigenous, and people of color (BIPOC) populations also tend to be the least resourced. Like BMC, they are safety-net hospitals serving primarily Medicaid or uninsured patients whose reimbursement rates are much lower than the rates for commercially insured patients. Nevertheless, safety-net hospitals need to make the additional investments that are required to deliver equitable care. Building a budget that can sustainably fund an equitable healthcare system must be a priority. This work can take many forms such as assuming more risk, fundraising through philanthropy and grants to propel innovation, and advocating with public and private payers for reimbursement models that support the investment needed to reduce inequities.

To transform the care at BMC, we sharply focused our lens on race and ethnicity across the health system. We created multidisciplinary working groups to interrogate clinical operations; identify high-inequity clinical areas; explore the impact of health-related social needs; and investigate how racism factors into our research, education, and workplace culture. These working groups have captured the patient and community voice in multiple surveys for each initiative, interviews, and community dialogues in partnership with a community advisory board.

The result of this work is our Health Equity Accelerator, a transformative approach to target the root causes of race-based health disparities, promote and sustain economic mobility, and end health inequities (Exhibit 1). The accelerator is a new kind of prescription, one that is not handed to our patients but instead handed internally to all leaders, staff members, nurses, physicians, and researchers throughout the health system.

ORGANIZATIONAL STRUCTURE

The task at hand for BMC, as part of a mission-driven integrated health system, is to improve outcomes for the Black, Hispanic, and Latino/a patients that make up our majority patient population in five key clinical areas with the most significant health inequities: pregnancy, infectious diseases (including COVID-19), chronic diseases (primarily diabetes and hypertension, as well as sickle cell anemia), behavioral health (mental health and substance use disorders [SUDs]), and cancer and end-stage renal disease.

Exhibit 1: Heath Equity Accelerator's First-Year Core Enablers and Multidisciplinary Teams

Multidisciplinary teams address priority clinical areas				
Equity in Pregnancy	COVID-19 Vaccine	Equity in Diabetes	Equity in Cancer	Behavioral Health (to be launched)

	Data	Culture	Community	SDOH	Research	Education	Advocacy
ENABLERS	Data collection, reporting, and infrastructure	DEI training and workforce development	Community and patient engagement	HRSN screener & referrals / Anchor network / Climate resiliency	Equity Research Team (an academic research approach must be central to our work)	Health Equity Fellowship (next generation equity leaders)	National and state level equity priorities / 1115 waiver, ACO program, and other procurements

Source: Boston Medical Center. © 2022. Used with permission.

Note: In its first year, 2021–2022, Boston Medical Center's Health Equity Accelerator built core enablers and launched multidisciplinary teams to address four of five priority clinical areas. ACO = accountable care organization; DEI = diversity, equity, and inclusion; HRSN = health-related social needs; SDOH = social determinants of health.

The organizational structure of the Health Equity Accelerator is the key to its effectiveness (Exhibit 2). At our academic medical center, we bring together investigators, clinicians, and experts from every facet of the system. These teams—one built for each of the five key clinical areas—form the heart of the Health Equity Accelerator.

Three institutional leaders direct the teams. Each leader brings a critical perspective to the work, including expertise in the principles of health equity, community engagement, and strategy. They ensure that initiatives align with institutional mission and community needs.

The clinical area teams meet biweekly to investigate inequities in the practices. As the team moves from discovery to implementation,

Exhibit 2: Example of Health Equity Accelerator Multidisciplinary Organizational Structure (Diabetes)

Senior leaders

Executive codirectors

Vice president of community engagement and external affairs

Priority clinical area team members (diabetes example)	Role
Clinical decision-makers	Medical director
	Community health center medical director
Clinical experts	Clinical lead
	Nursing lead
	Nutritionist
	Pharmacist
Research experts	Researchers
	Research methodology expert
	Medical librarian
	Data analytics expert
Operational experts	Clinical operations representative
	Social needs expert
	Patient navigator
	Human resources/culture expert
Health equity experts	Program manager
	Strategy/learning health system expert
	Community engagement expert
	Patient engagement expert

more experts are added to the core team to help carry out solutions. Our analytics team leverages clinical and claims data plus data from our survey of patient needs and other external public health data points to uncover racial and ethnic trends and relationships that may not be obvious.

With everyone at the table, we generate hypotheses through primary research (extensive surveys, interviews, focus groups with patients) and existing literature.

FIVE PRINCIPLES THAT PERPETUATE INEQUITY

Rapid action to holistically address the inequities we uncover is paramount to our approach to equitable care. In developing the Health Equity Accelerator, we have learned five principles that apply to all clinical areas and disproportionally affect patients in marginalized communities by perpetuating cycles of health inequities. These principles are informing our prescriptions to align the goals of our established work to close health gaps. These principles, described in the following sections, can be guideposts for other institutions undertaking health equity work.

1. Wealth Is Health

Centuries of discriminatory policies (e.g., redlining) have raised significant barriers to a life trajectory of thriving in communities of color, limiting access to jobs, housing, education, and pathways to wealth building. A groundbreaking report (Muñoz et al. 2015) revealed a staggering divide: Black families in Boston had a median net worth of only $8 compared to $247,000 for white Bostonians. To break the generational cycles of poverty and poor health, we are embracing the power of BMC's role as an anchor institution to support the community with initiatives like StreetCred (described in the sidebar).

Creating Living Wage Jobs and Career Pathways

BMC is part of an integrated health system that employs approximately 10,000 people. We recognize our leading role in improving economic development in the communities we serve. In 2017, we became the first hospital to participate in the BostonHires program, a city-led movement to connect residents to employment opportunities. As a partner with other anchor institutions and community organizations, we apply a place-based approach to recruit, train, and employ people from historically underinvested neighborhoods surrounding our campus. A grant from JPMorgan Chase as a part of its Advancing Cities Challenge has enabled us to hire more than 600 people from the community.

In addition, we are working to fast-track career advancement for employees of color within our health system through a six-month leadership acceleration program. The training program connects top-performing employees with career coaches, mentors, and career navigators to help them transition into management roles in our health system. We recently completed our fourth cohort of the program.

STREETCRED: BUILDING WEALTH TO IMPROVE HEALTH

In 2016, a mother's request for tax preparation help in the BMC pediatric waiting room sparked an innovative solution to put money back into the pockets of families who cannot afford to lose it. Two BMC pediatricians who heard about the mother's request for help were moved to develop StreetCred, a free in-hospital tax preparation service that now returns nearly $1 million annually to Boston families (www.mystreetcred.org).

StreetCred exemplifies the holistic way BMC targets the social ills of poverty, housing instability, and hunger—the main drivers of poor health that cannot always be addressed clinically.

For example, the federal earned income tax credit (EITC) and expanded child tax credit can provide an average of $2,000–$3,000 a year to eligible low- to middle-income families, which is enough for about six months of groceries. Yet many families (like those led by the young mother in the BMC pediatric waiting room) are unable to claim their EITC on their own and must find hundreds of dollars to pay for the services of a professional tax preparer.

The Health Equity Accelerator has prioritized the expansion of StreetCred's bundled-model approach, which systematically offers financial coaching and enrollment support for 529 college savings plan accounts, in addition to tax preparation. Together, the services foster financial literacy and wealth building. StreetCred, which is now offered in nine states and Washington, DC, recently launched the Medical Tax Collaborative (MTC) to build a wider movement toward incorporating financial well-being into healthcare. The MTC provides technical support to hospitals and health clinics that want to launch their own medical–financial partnership programs.

Partnering with BIPOC Business Owners

BMC spends $2 billion annually on supplies and services, and we are working to ensure equity when sourcing and purchasing from these vendors. Our supply chain department operationalizes intentionality to purchase from women- and minority-owned vendors. We report on the data monthly to an internal committee that monitors progress.

Improving Health Through Affordable Housing

Better housing is preventive medicine at its best. Since 2017, BMC has invested $6.5 million to improve community health with more affordable, supportive, and stable housing. For example, in 2017 BMC launched a collaboration with Boston Children's Hospital and Brigham and Women's Hospital to identify, assess, and fund strategic approaches to increase housing stability for vulnerable populations. BMC also invested in an affordable housing development that has committed to providing 60 supportive housing units for individuals with complex medical needs.

These investments have been funded in part through the Massachusetts Determination of Need (DoN) process. Health systems that undertake campus renovations are required to direct a portion of the cost into investments in community projects. In 2017, during our campus consolidation, we allocated our DoN funding obligation to increase Boston's inventory of supportive housing units.

Investing in Neighborhood Economies

To build a strong ecosystem of inclusive wealth building and economic mobility, BMC is investing in local BIPOC businesses to grow and hire locally. For example, as part of our DoN obligation, we provided a $1 million no-interest loan to a supermarket in a new affordable housing complex in the Roxbury neighborhood. The full-service halal market provides fresh produce and food to a community with few accessible grocery chain options. With the loan, we advocated for the operators to be owners of the business and the physical space. We also advocated for living-wage salaries for the employees and employee equity ownership in the business.

2. Time Is a Luxury

Disease prevention and health management can take the time that BIPOC populations do not have. A survey found that 64 percent of Black children live in single-parent households (Annie E. Casey Foundation 2022), and many of these parents work multiple jobs or shifts that leave few hours to prioritize healthcare. A doctor's visit means taking a half day or more off from work; a diagnosis may require multiple clinical visits and long processes with insurance companies to qualify for treatment. Chronic conditions such as diabetes and hypertension present special challenges for patients who cannot closely monitor their disease or take off work for appointments.

Missed routine care, screenings, and delays in procedures are disproportionately costing Black and brown patients and leading to worse health outcomes. The Health Equity Accelerator is forging new pathways to reduce the time required for patients to invest in their health. In times of crisis, this means meeting patients where they are. In day-to-day clinical practice, it means pinpointing how we can make care more convenient and better streamlined for our patients. Some examples follow:

- **Expanded access to care.** In 2020, BMC cared for consecutive surges of the sickest COVID-19 patients in greater Boston—not surprising, given that many people in the communities we serve are essential workers who cannot shelter in place and live in crowded, multigenerational households. When the vaccine first became available, we quickly recognized the emerging "vaccine access desert" in these hard-hit communities. We partnered with community organizations and government agencies to stand up five vaccination sites at our community healthcare centers early in the rollout. We made sure there was a vaccination site within a mile of everyone in our catchment area. Beyond that, we added a mobile unit that has held more than 400 pop-up vaccination events as a partner with Boston Public Schools and YMCAs in areas with high concentrations of unvaccinated patients. This inclusive approach increased equity in vaccine distribution. As of September 2022, 63 percent of patients vaccinated at BMC and our community vaccination sites have been people of color, compared with 31 percent of people of color vaccinated throughout Massachusetts.

- **Innovation through new time-saving technology.**
Many of BMC's excess cases of severe maternal morbidity among Black patients have been the result of variations in the management of preeclampsia. To address this, our obstetrics and gynecology department is launching interventions to build patient agency around preeclampsia (e.g., doula expansion, multicultural preeclampsia education, a website chatbot), tighten protocols to reduce variation in timing, retrain staff to better partner with patients in decision-making, and provide remote blood pressure cuffs to high-risk pregnant patients. The technology enables nurses and physicians to identify serious changes in blood pressure earlier while expectant and new mothers stay at home. The intervention is showing promising results with high patient engagement—the rate of any hypertension-identified postpartum for the first 1,000 patients using devices was 64 percent, double the rate reported in other studies (Mujic, Parker, and Yarrington 2022). Similar studies are underway using cellular glucometers to remotely monitor patients who are at risk for gestational diabetes.

3. Agency Is Essential

When patients feel that a healthcare decision or procedure is done *to* them, not *for* them, they lose a sense of safety and trust in the system. This loss can affect future patient–provider communication and result in delays and differences in care.

Mistrust of the health system will endure until a more culturally adept and relatable approach is found. The Health Equity Accelerator team has identified a three-pronged approach to the problem.

Bolster Cultural Responsiveness

We are working to be a trusted resource that aligns culturally with patients' information needs and empowers them in complex health situations where there is a lot to learn. Beyond enriching the BMC healthcare team's ability to empower patients across healthcare settings, we are providing more culturally and linguistically inclusive patient support.

For example, we found vast disparities in severe maternal morbidity between Black and white pregnant patients. As part of our response, we expanded our Birth Sisters program, which offers women "sisterlike" doula support during pregnancy and through the postpartum period. Our multicultural doulas have improved birth outcomes, breastfeeding rates, and the experience of care (as indicated in patient surveys). Black patients with birth sisters have fewer cesarean sections and more exclusive breastfeeding during delivery hospitalization compared to Black patients without birth sisters, and patients (regardless of race) with birth sisters have babies at a higher gestational age at birth and fewer neonatal intensive care unit admissions compared to patients without birth sisters. With this encouraging data and grant-funded support, BMC is hiring and training more women from the community to expand the doula service.

Confront Racism in the Workforce

Confronting implicit and explicit bias and racist attitudes within the healthcare workforce is essential to transform care. Working hard to implant diversity, equity, and inclusion (DEI) into the organizational DNA at BMC, we have created and embedded a culture code. The code includes basic behaviors for everyday encounters, such as "Make it a 5-star hello" and "STOP (See The Other Person)," to help staff authentically engage, set aside snap judgments, and incorporate DEI into all interactions. We are conducting training that includes this new framework as well as many tools for intervention throughout the campus to help teams grow in self-awareness and deliver excellence.

Ensure Representation in Medicine

Commitments to equity, engagement, and cultural representation at all levels and patient touchpoints are essential to building patient trust. We take this seriously in multiple ways at BMC, from unique advancement programs that increase diversity in our hospital workforce and leadership to boosting recruitment efforts of underrepresented in medicine (URiM) trainees in residency and fellowship programs.

Academic medical centers play a crucial role in supporting the matriculation and career development of medical students of color. Nationally, only 13 percent of active US clinical residents self-identify as Black or Hispanic (Accreditation Council for Graduate Medical Education 2021), which means that they are URiM. Despite BMC's diverse patient population, the racial diversity of our residency training programs has historically been equal to or less than the national median (Wusu et al. 2019). To grow a more diverse physician workforce, we set a goal of at least 20 percent of URiM residents and fellows. In the 2022 academic year, we recruited the highest percentage of URiM intern classes ever at 29 percent, and the highest number of overall URiM trainees (residents and fellows) at 21 percent.

4. Timing Is Everything

In studying racial inequities, the Health Equity Accelerator team found mounting evidence that inequities in outcomes stem more frequently from differences in the timing of care than from differences in the quality of care. For example, many excess cases of severe maternal morbidity among Black patients at BMC resulted from variations in the management of preeclampsia, as described earlier. Delays in diagnosis or treatment result in an increased risk of complications and mortality.

We have determined that when there is no clear goal on how long something should take, it takes longer for BIPOC patients.

From diagnoses to the start of treatment, ambiguity in process breeds discrimination. Tightening protocols is the quickest, most impactful way to reduce disparities in health outcomes. BMC departments are now expected to review decisions that are time sensitive and set standardized goals for the timing of those decisions.

Rethinking Decision to Incision

As part of BMC's quality improvement work in 2019, we uncovered the fact that our Black patients were waiting significantly longer for urgent cesarean sections than our white patients. In response, we created a decision-to-incision metric for the department. Standardization of this protocol helped to address process bias and worked to reduce the time disparity between Black and white patients substantially (Mendez-Escobar et al. 2022).

Dialing in on Our Approach to Diabetes

We are also stressing the importance of timing in our Equity in Diabetes initiative. We have learned how delays in treatment may contribute to inequities in diabetes management. A national study reported that only 10.4 percent of patients with a diagnosis of prediabetes had a coded diagnosis of prediabetes, only 1.0 percent were referred for nutrition, and only 5.4 percent were prescribed metformin despite clinical practice guidelines to do so. Further, Black individuals were 1.4 times more likely to develop diabetes than white individuals (Tseng et al. 2022). The Health Equity Accelerator team is working to understand and apply tighter protocols of prediabetes management in primary care at BMC.

5. Averages Are Blind

Many national guidelines and beliefs in medicine are based on population averages that do not apply to all subgroups, and we at BMC have long known that our BIPOC patients face unique health challenges. In building the Health Equity Accelerator, we addressed the need to systematically identify what matters to BIPOC patients to a disproportionately greater degree than national averages, and we continue to specialize our care to improve their outcomes. We acknowledge and embrace race as part of health.

Promoting Excellence in Sickle Cell Disease Care
In a US population of nearly 330 million, sickle cell disease is typically classified as rare. Drilling down, however, 1 in 13 Black Americans carry the sickle cell trait, making the incidence of the disease much higher in predominantly Black communities. Many health systems still lack protocols to care for patients with sickle cell disease who come to the hospital in excruciating pain. Long wait times, inadequate care, and continued discrimination serve to perpetuate poor health outcomes and reduce life expectancy. Through BMC's Center of Excellence in Sickle Cell Disease, we have created, and continue to expand, models of care and protocols that ensure proper multispecialty care from birth through adulthood for patients and expedite pain management for patients who are experiencing acute sickle cell crises.

Prioritizing Prostate Cancer
Frequently, cancer screening projects deprioritize prostate cancer because, generally, it can be well managed and has a low mortality rate. That may be true on average, but for Black men, the death rate of prostate cancer is more than two times higher than for white men (American Cancer Society 2022). With a dedicated multicultural outreach team, we are launching an effort to increase cancer screening rates.

Expanding Treatment Options for Substance Abuse Disorder (SUD)
BMC is at the forefront of addiction care. We pioneered office-based addiction treatment, now the key to nationally scaled opioid addiction treatment in primary care. Working to quell the opioid crisis with medications has been a top priority.

However, we found that 67 percent of our Black patients have SUDs unrelated to opioids and therefore need different treatment options. Although more than 90 percent of patients with opioid use disorder are engaged in outpatient treatment, this number is much smaller for patients with other SUDs. Over the past two years, we have expanded psychotherapy (the most effective outpatient option for nonopioid SUDs) and other treatment options to close disparities in care. To provide more equitable care, we recently opened an 82-bed inpatient care facility in Brockton, Massachusetts. The new facility cares for co-occurring psychiatric and SUD disorders and addresses a critical shortage of behavioral health inpatient beds. The new facility is a pivotal resource to help our patients with SUD toward long-term recovery.

CONCLUSION

Launching the Health Equity Accelerator has been a humbling and clarifying experience at BMC. We embrace our role, both inside our organization and outside our walls, as a community leader in rethinking the delivery of care. The stakes are high. With unflinching focus, strong partnerships, and investment priorities, we have defined the work ahead that is required to address inequities. Using five principles as guideposts—wealth is health, time is a luxury, agency is essential, timing is everything, and averages are blind—we created a prescription that we believe can also catalyze change at other healthcare organizations.

As communities continue to grow in diversity, the health systems that serve them must also evolve and relinquish antiquated one-size-fits-all approaches to care. Race is part of health, and care systems must embrace and address that reality. By adopting that social obligation, we at BMC are expanding our efforts to help wipe out appalling health disparities so that all patients can live healthy lives.

ACKNOWLEDGMENTS

Thea James, MD, executive director of the Health Equity Accelerator and vice president of mission and associate CMO at Boston Medical Center Health System, and Elena Mendez-Escobar, PhD, executive director of the Health Equity Accelerator and executive director of strategy at Boston Medical Center Health System, made significant contributions to this article.

REFERENCES

Accreditation Council for Graduate Medical Education. 2021. "Number of Active MD Residents, by Race/Ethnicity (Alone or In Combination) and GME Specialty." Accessed October 18, 2022. https://www.aamc.org/data-reports/students-residents /interactivedata/report-residents/2020/table-b5-mdresidents -race-ethnicity-and-specialty.

American Cancer Society. 2022. "Cancer Statistics for African American/Black People 2022–2024." https://www.cancer.org /content/dam/cancer-org/research/cancer-facts-andstatistics /cancer-facts-and-figures-for-africanamericans/2022-2024-cff -aa.pdf.

Annie E. Casey Foundation. 2022. "Child Well-Being in Single-Parent Families." https://www.aecf.org/blog/child-well-being -in-single-parent-families.

Boston Medical Center. 2021. "The Health Equity Accelerator: The Next Step in Our Commitment to Equity." https://www.bmc.org /sites/default/files/2022-03/Report_Final_Interactive_update _2.15.22_0.pdf.

Bovell-Ammon, A., C. Mansilla, A. Poblacion, L. Rateau, T. Heeren, J. T. Cook, T. Zhang, S. Ettinger de Cuba, and M. T. Sandel. 2020. "Housing Intervention for Medically Complex Families Associated with Improved Family Health: Pilot Randomized Trial." *Health Affairs* 39 (4): 613–21. https://www.healthaffairs.org/doi/pdf/10.1377/hlthaff.2019.01569.

Mendez-Escobar, E., T. M. Adegoke, A. Lee-Parritz, J. Spangler, S. A. Wilson, C. Yarrington, Z. Xuan, A. Bell, and T. James. 2022. "Health Equity Accelerator: A Health System's Approach." *NEJM Catalyst*. Published June 7, 2022. https://doi.org/10.1056/CAT.22.0115.

Mujic, E., S. Parker, and C. Yarrington. 2022. "Abstract EP50: Implementation of a Cloud-Connected Remote Blood Pressure Monitoring Program During the Postpartum Period Improves Ascertainment." *Circulation*. Published April 7, 2022. https://doi.org/10.1161/circ.145.suppl_1.EP50.

Muñoz, A. P., M. Kim, M. Chang, R. O. Jackson, D. Hamilton, and W. A. Darity Jr. 2015. "The Color of Wealth in Boston." Duke University, The New School, and the Federal Reserve Bank of Boston. Published March 25, 2015. https://www.bostonfed.org/publications/one-timepubs/color-of-wealth.aspx.

Tseng, E., N. Durkin, J. M. Clark, N. M. Maruthur, J. A. Marsteller, and J. B. Segal. 2022. "Clinical Care Among Individuals with Prediabetes in Primary Care: A Retrospective Cohort Study." *Journal of General Internal Medicine*. Published March 2, 2022. 1–8. https://doi.org/10.1007/s11606-022-07412-9.

Wusu, M. H., S. Tepperberg, J. M. Weinberg, and R. B. Saper. 2019. "Matching Our Mission: A Strategic Plan to Create a Diverse Family Medicine Residency." *Family Medicine* 51 (1): 31–36. https://doi.org/10.22454/FamMed.2019.955445.

FOR DISCUSSION

1. Boston Medical Center is a safety-net hospital with a good reputation for quality. So why would leadership be so concerned about falling short of its mission to serve its community?
2. How can healthcare organizations "think beyond the pill bottle" to improve access to care?
3. What is the Health Equity Accelerator at Boston Medical Center? How can it be replicated?
4. What can be the result if a patient feels a healthcare decision or procedure is done *to* them, not *for* them?

LOWN INSTITUTE: MEASURING WHAT MATTERS

More and more hospitals are walking the talk when it comes to social responsibility. Their forward movement is driven by new methods for measuring hospital performance to which they can be held accountable. It's a challenging but exciting time for the healthcare sector.

How can this evolving movement be scaled up? By analyzing big data across 54 different metrics and publishing the results, the Lown Institute is working to raise the standard for hospital social responsibility.

Hospitals are uniquely positioned to lead on social responsibility because of the multiple roles they serve within their communities. They are not only healthcare providers but also employers, purchasers, political actors, and part of the physical environment of their neighborhoods. The decisions hospital leaders make—how they invest in local health initiatives and community organizations, whom they welcome into the hospital and onto their board, and how much they pay their workers—have a great impact on the well-being of their community.

Building Community, Improving Health

When hospitals build community health programs around housing, education, and food security, they can improve health from earliest childhood. Ensuring that care is accessible to all regardless of income, race, ethnicity, or insurance status helps reduce healthcare disparities. And paying employees fairly boosts financial security in the community, which benefits both health outcomes and local economic vitality.

The growth of environmental, social, and governance (ESG) products in the financial sector has propelled the movement further. More than $50 billion flowed into sustainable funds in 2020, nearly *10 times* the amount just 2 years prior (Hale 2021). At the same time, conflicting definitions of ESG and concerns about greenwashing (businesses using marketing to burnish their image without making any real change) have led to scrutiny and regulatory action. The Securities and Exchange Commission will be adopting new standards for ESG disclosures for publicly traded companies to ensure that they include "material, decision-useful" information on ESG (Lee 2022). As the ESG movement continues, access to metrics that are clear, meaningful, and trustworthy is increasingly important.

Hospitals that have made commitments to confront racism in their institutions, reduce health disparities in their communities, and invest in programs to improve social drivers of health need to ensure that these sentiments translate into accountable action. The Lown Hospitals Index for Social Responsibility (www .lownhospitalsindex.org) evaluates 54 measures across equity, value, and outcomes to help hospital leaders track progress on social responsibility and identify opportunities for improvement (Exhibit 1). Besides setting ambitious goals for the sector, the index honors the hospitals that are leading the movement toward social responsibility with top grades.

Index metrics include:

- inclusivity, which measures how well a hospital's patient population reflects the racial and socioeconomic demographics of the community surrounding it;
- community benefit, which measures investments with direct local impact by reporting on hospital spending on financial assistance and community health investments, as well as hospitals' service of Medicaid patients; and

Exhibit 1: The Lown Hospitals Index Tree

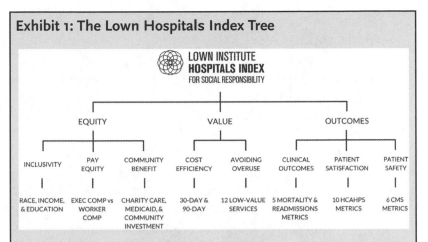

Source: The Lown Institute. Used with permission.

Note: The Lown Institute Hospitals Index includes metrics across health equity, value, and outcomes to create a ranking of hospital social responsibility.

- pay equity, which measures how much hospitals' senior executives are compensated compared to hospital workers without advanced degrees.

The results of the Lown Hospitals Index also illuminate systemic barriers to health equity. For example, many major metro areas in the United States have racially segregated hospital systems, driven in part by a reimbursement system that pays less for publicly insured patients compared to privately insured ones (Garber 2022). Similarly, the lack of regulations on community benefit allows some hospitals to give back much less than others. Through its reports, convenings, and partnerships, the Lown Institute arms hospitals and policymakers with the data needed to align financial and regulatory incentives toward social responsibility.

Striving to Do Good

For Lown Institute founder Bernard Lown, MD, it wasn't enough for doctors to care for their patients. He believed that they also had to advocate for the health of humanity. Since the Lown Hospitals Index was launched in 2020, many hospitals have embraced Dr. Lown's expansive vision of the role of medicine by building social responsibility into their goals and sharing their performance along the way. In this way, hospitals can be not just providers of high-quality care but also champions for equity and contributors to community well-being. They know it's not enough to do no harm, they also know that they must strive to do good.

Lown Institute

REFERENCES

Garber, J. 2022. "America's Failure to Integrate Hospitals." *Anti-Racism Daily.* Published March 17, 2022. https://the-ard.com/2022/03/17/the-lasting-impact-of-racial-segregation-in-hospitals/.

Hale, J. 2021. "A Broken Record: Flows for U.S. Sustainable Funds Again Reach New Heights." Morningstar. Published January 28, 2021. https://www.morningstar.com/articles/1019195/a-broken-record-flowsfor-us-sustainable-funds-again-reach-newheights.

Lee, A. H. 2022. "SEC: Public Input Welcomed on Climate Change Disclosures." Accessed September 27, 2022. https://www.sec.gov/news/public-statement/lee-climate-change-disclosures.

Community Health Improvement: Social Care Is Healthcare

EMILY KRYZER, MSW, MPH, AND
CHRISTOPHER M. NOLAN, FACHE

SUMMARY

Like many communities across the United States, St. Louis, Missouri, faces stark inequities in health outcomes, including wellness, quality of life, and life expectancy. These inequities are the result of social systems and policies that have robbed generations of St. Louisans of opportunity. BJC HealthCare's (BJC's) commitment to becoming a catalyst for community health by helping to eliminate health disparities led to the launch of its community health improvement strategy. This article details the community-driven and evidence-informed process that BJC used to create a multiyear, proactive approach to addressing the social and economic factors that are the root causes of health inequities. It examines areas of opportunity through which the strategy will drive change and explores lessons learned and promising practices for other healthcare institutions to consider as they advance health equity.

In St. Louis, Missouri, health is not equally distributed. One of the most-cited findings in describing the health of the St. Louis region is an 18-year gap in life expectancy at birth between people who are born in two zip codes separated by less than 10 miles (Purnell et al. 2014). Place matters in St. Louis, as it does in cities throughout the country (Harper et al. 2014; Holder and Montgomery 2019; King et al. 2022). Place matters because it shapes St. Louisans' access to social and economic resources, including income, education, quality neighborhoods, transportation, and basic social services. The history of a place also matters. In St. Louis, the history of racial segregation—and decades of local, state, and federal policies that reinforced structural racism—has left a mark on the health and well-being of all St. Louisans (Cambria et al. 2018; Gordon 2008; Rothstein 2014). In the two disparate zip codes, the most notable differences are poverty level and racial composition. In one community (78 percent White), the life expectancy is 85 years and only 7 percent of the population lives below the poverty line. In the other community (95 percent Black), the life expectancy is 67 years and more than half (54 percent) of its population lives in poverty.

The link between segregation and health is clear: Concentrating poverty at the neighborhood level limits access to critical resources and opportunities, and the result is poorer health, education, and other life outcomes (Kramer and Hogue 2009).

CONSCIOUS CHOICES OF OUR PAST

How can a large healthcare system begin to confront the region's history and create a new narrative in which all can live a long, productive, and healthy life? The answer to this question for BJC HealthCare (BJC), a large nonprofit integrated academic health system, has come down to changing decisions made, leveraging power and resources in new ways, and expanding the role of healthcare providers in addressing the root causes of health inequities. Through an enhanced commitment to community health improvement,

BJC is making an intentional change to address disparities inside and outside of its walls. After all, public health research has confirmed that health and well-being, including premature death, are driven predominantly by socioeconomic conditions, not medical care (Braveman and Gottlieb 2014; Schroeder 2007).

As Cambria and colleagues (2018, 12) observe, "Conscious choices created our 'geography of inequity' in St. Louis. Conscious choices can also help to reshape it." The fatal shooting of Michael Brown in Ferguson, Missouri, in August 2014 was a critical inflection point, accelerating the need for the conscious undoing of systemic racism and its effects in St. Louis. This event, and the unrest that followed, brought to light the health and social inequities. Since that time, and especially during the COVID-19 pandemic, community members, organizations, and institutions in St. Louis have worked to confront the role that race plays in shaping unequal outcomes. Organizations in each sector, from education to housing to healthcare, continue to forge new paths for broader racial equity. It is on this foundation that BJC is able to work collaboratively with the community toward a St. Louis where geography and race do not determine outcomes.

A FRAMEWORK FOR ADDRESSING DISPARITIES

BJC has a long-standing commitment to improving the health of the communities it serves, and it made an enhanced commitment to address health disparities in 2019 when it articulated a vision for its emergence as a national leader among integrated healthcare delivery organizations (BJC HealthCare 2021). The vision consists of four areas of focus: community health improvement, clinical quality, customer centricity, and financial stability. The launch of BJC's Community Health Improvement Team in 2020 signaled an additional emphasis on being a catalyst for health and well-being. It also presented an opportunity to work at the intersection of healthcare, economics, and social care to address persistent inequities in health.

As the Community Health Improvement Team set out to launch a strategic planning process, it established a framework to illustrate how BJC can promote health equity and have a meaningful impact on community health. This framework includes three pillars:

- **Anchor institution strategy.** The first pillar seeks to leverage BJC's role as the largest employer in the St. Louis region and a major purchaser of local goods and services, as well as a major investor.
- **Community partnership and collaboration.** The second pillar recognizes BJC's need to partner with community members who are most directly affected by health inequities and the institutions that serve them. Through equitable partnerships and collaboration, BJC can more effectively leverage existing resources and infrastructure and, most importantly, cocreate more impactful solutions with the community.
- **Policy to address social determinants of health.** The third pillar supports the role that policy—at all levels—plays in transforming systems and communities. Without policy interventions that bring solutions to scale, it would be difficult for BJC or any single actor to implement the population-level changes needed to eliminate disparities.

A STRATEGIC PLANNING PROCESS

With this framework as its guide, and with support from executive leadership, BJC began a nine-month strategic planning process that engaged more than 200 internal and external stakeholders. The planning process (described later) was informed by both public health and community expertise (BJC HealthCare 2021) gathered through:

- key informational interviews with BJC leaders, academic and public health partners, community and social service providers, and elected officials (23 interviews);
- listening and learning sessions with groups of stakeholders within BJC's system who are most heavily engaged in the organization's existing community health efforts, including social workers, nurses, board members, and other health professionals (6 sessions, 120 individuals);
- steering committee planning sessions with internal and external stakeholders who developed the mission, vision, and guiding principles for the Community Health Improvement Team's efforts (4 sessions, 20 individuals); and
- working group planning sessions with internal and external content experts, including public policy experts and members of community-based organizations who developed the priorities, goals, and measures of success for each focus area of the strategic plan (5 sessions for each area, 70 individuals).

The mission developed by the steering committee describes the purpose of the Community Health Improvement Team's work as well as whom it serves and how it will execute its purpose:

BJC Community Health Improvement advances health equity for those most impacted by health disparities in the urban and rural communities that BJC serves through authentic and equitable partnerships with community stakeholders and community members.

The group's vision for success—"a thriving bistate region in which all people have an equal opportunity to live their healthiest lives"—underscores that health equity is not just an outcome but rather a process of transforming the social and economic conditions that produce predictable health disparities around race, income, gender, and geography. Steering committee members also identified the following principles to inform how BJC makes decisions, allocates resources, and implements its community health improvement strategy (BJC HealthCare 2021):

- **Center health equity.** By centering health equity, BJC will ensure that everything it does is in service of the well-being of communities that have endured disinvestment and discrimination. This work includes providing disproportionate resources to those who have suffered the greatest harm and resolving the root causes and conditions that drive health disparities.
- **Partner authentically and equitably.** Recognizing that community health improvement is not the work of a single individual, organization, or system, BJC will reject siloed efforts; listen to humbly, learn from, and value the leadership of impacted communities; work with institutions and individuals who are on the front lines of service; and build bridges with those who do not share BJC's perspective or agenda. Importantly, BJC will also negotiate resource and power imbalances that have contributed to disparities.
- **Focus on the long term.** BJC understands that the transformation it seeks requires a generational approach. To sustain this change, BJC will exercise more creativity and informed risk-taking as well as greater investment in community capacity and infrastructure.
- **Maintain accountability.** BJC's accountability to the communities it serves requires that it review important decisions, actions, and impacts with stakeholders, and truthfully report successes and shortcomings. BJC will also act on what it learns, including when it has not operated in alignment with its principles.

PRIORITIES, PARTNERS, AND MEASURES OF SUCCESS

BJC's strategic planning partners identified areas of opportunity for the Community Health Improvement Team's efforts. Each area was organized around a central aim and its priorities. Priorities were determined collaboratively among working groups. The groups assessed each potential priority to identify the greatest promise for providing the most to those most adversely affected by existing social, economic, and health conditions (equity); transforming conditions for the better (impact); being maintained and escalated over time by BJC or its partners (sustainability); aligning with BJC's expertise, capacity, and resources (capacity); and building on the work of others who are executing effective and coordinated action (existing efforts). Although not described in detail here, specific goals, objectives, and strategies were also established for each focus area of the strategic plan (Exhibit 1).

BJC HealthCare's community health improvement strategic plan covers each area with four specific priorities and goals:

Exhibit 1: BJC HealthCare's Community Health Improvement Strategic Plan

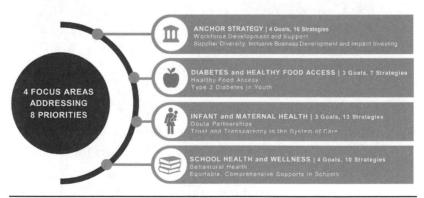

Source: BJC HealthCare © 2021. Used with permission.

- **Anchor strategy.** BJC aims to close the racial wage and wealth gaps to improve individual and community-level health outcomes. The priorities are workforce development and support (hiring, promoting, and retaining Black employees; creating opportunities through pipeline programs) and supplier diversity, including business development, and impact investing (supporting the growth of Black-owned businesses, investing in local community and economic development).
- **Diabetes and healthy food access.** BJC aims to reduce racial disparities in diabetes incidence and prevalence by improving access to healthy food and physical activity. BJC will prioritize efforts that address healthy food access (improving awareness of and access to healthy and affordable food, investing in community food ownership models) and type 2 diabetes in youth (amplifying successful intergenerational nutrition and physical activity programs).
- **Infant and maternal health.** BJC aims to improve Black infant and maternal health outcomes by ensuring trust and transparency and providing culturally appropriate, holistic clinical care. Priorities are doula partnerships (supporting the integration of doulas in clinical settings, introducing families to doulas early in their pregnancy, and developing mechanisms to reimburse doulas) and improving trust and transparency in the system of care (growing and retaining Black clinical care team members, collecting and sharing stories of patient experiences, and advocating for community-facing data systems).
- **School health and wellness.** BJC aims to advance equitable health and educational outcomes by increasing access to comprehensive wraparound support for children and staff in early learning and K–12 settings and in surrounding communities. Priorities are behavioral health (increasing support for school- and community-based behavioral health programs, increasing the capacity of

schools to bill Medicaid for behavioral health services) and equitable and comprehensive support in schools (adopting the Centers for Disease Control and Prevention's Whole School, Whole Community, Whole Child model and increasing knowledge and use of trauma-informed services that are culturally relevant).

WHAT WORKS, WHAT DOESN'T

As BJC deepens its commitment through strategic action and support, the Community Health Improvement Team is learning lessons that other healthcare organizations may apply to their journeys, including recommendations for what not to do.

The first nine months of BJC's community health improvement strategic plan brought to light the importance of partnership and power in creating the kind of deep and trusting relationships needed to do this work; the iterative and collaborative process used to develop initial measures of success; and the opportunities through which connections can be made across the system.

Partnerships, Roles, and Power

Partnership and collaboration are vital to achieving the long-term potential of each of the four community health improvement strategic focus areas. Making the most of existing momentum and infrastructure requires understanding where and when BJC needs to lead versus the need to step back and follow others.

In the planning process, BJC identified core roles that it can play during strategy execution (Exhibit 2). Some tasks (e.g., supporting the integration of doulas in clinical settings) require the Community Health Improvement Team to initiate and guide action as the leader. Other tasks (e.g., increasing support for school- and community-based behavioral health programs) are better suited to the roles of investor, champion, and amplifier, in which the team follows the lead of others in the community. Being intentional about the role taken not only extends BJC's capacity but also creates the space to show up in the community in new and more equitable ways. Equally important is the ability to be nimble. As projects unfold, roles often shift to meet the needs of collaborators and projects. For example, the Community Health Improvement Team first positioned itself internally to lead the development of a regional data hub to increase transparency regarding infant and maternal health outcomes, only to realize that another community partner was getting ready to launch a similar community-facing data initiative. The team's role quickly shifted from setting the table (leader) to bringing other health systems to the table (champion, amplifier).

Exhibit 2: Central Roles in BJC's Community Health Improvement Efforts

Leader	Initiates and guides collective action to achieve desired community outcomes
Partner	Cocreates initiatives along with a set of strategic partners, sharing resources and capacities for mutual benefit and meaningful impact
Investor	Invests money and possibly other needed resources into plans, with the expectation of achieving a significant impact
Champion	Listens to, learns from, and actively promotes organizations that are leading impactful work on the priority
Amplifier	Increases the power and visibility of efforts so that actions and impacts can be brought to scale
Convener	Calls stakeholders together to engage in aligned, coordinated action; provides support to the collective as it works to advance shared interests and agendas
Policy advocate	Works to influence the legislative and administrative actions of decision-makers

As the team has learned, the work of community health improvement requires not only leadership but also followership. It is not only impossible to be the leader of every strategy, it is unwarranted. To be successful, health systems must show up in new ways in the community and model the values of those roles, including humility, mutuality, and allyship. When BJC shows up for partnership discussions, it is almost always one of the largest organizations in the room. That does not mean it knows best. Practical steps to achieving more balanced power dynamics start with listening and being open and honest about roles.

The team also acknowledges that some relationships take longer to build than others and need varying levels of attention to maintain and grow, particularly in areas in which there is a history of distrust or reluctance to collaborate with large organizations. Additionally, BJC has an overarching understanding of the activities taking place throughout the region. This allows the team to identify synergy points and serve as a connector between organizations to help accelerate shared goals and maximize impact.

Measuring Success

As noted earlier, BJC focuses on the long term. This requires seemingly paradoxical thinking: Understanding that the transformational change envisioned is generational in scope and scale while acting on present and urgent needs. As an education partner remarked when describing the immediate need for more behavioral health supports, "Our house is on fire, *now*."

This challenge comes to the forefront when determining how to measure success. As part of the strategic planning process, each working group identified an initial set of measures, including short-term and long-term outcomes as well as process-related (e.g., the quantity of a service delivered) and impact-related (e.g., changes in conditions) outcomes. The working groups consulted public health literature to understand what outcomes were plausible. Engaging community members and organizations throughout the process helped to ensure that selected outcomes reflected what true success looks like to those most affected.

The Community Health Improvement Team continues to evaluate the initial set of measures and has developed dashboards for each of the four strategic focus areas. Each dashboard features two to three indicators with established yearly targets and year-to-date progress in achieving the targets. Policy and partnership milestones, such as advocacy efforts, new community partnerships, and outcomes from coalition meetings, are also detailed on the dashboard.

The team prioritized each indicator through a process that included evaluating whether the data for the indicator existed, whether the indicator supported equity (i.e., aimed at a population or region that has been disproportionately affected by health disparities), and whether the work would move the needle toward the target. In some instances, data for the indicator were not available. When acceptable proxies were available, they were used; when they were not, the creation of the indicator became the indicator itself.

Some of the short-term indicators for each focus area include

- total spend with minority- and women-owned businesses in priority zip codes in the St. Louis region (anchor strategy);
- average change in A1c among patients with uncontrolled diabetes who are food insecure and receive culturally and medically appropriate meals (diabetes and healthy food access);
- development of a plan for an electronic health record–integrated data system to monitor the use of doulas across BJC facilities (infant and maternal health);
- number of community wellness hubs operating in partnership with community organizations (school health and wellness); and
- total community financial investments in each area.

Creating meaningful measurements for this work requires iteration, trusting relationships with partners, and an adaptive mindset. The indicators will likely change as knowledge increases and the work unfolds. Getting to the right measures takes time.

A recommendation for what *not* to do is simple: Don't go at it alone. All the work involves some level of partnership. For some strategic focus areas, BJC is building on years of work, which allows teams to leverage measures that are known and accepted by the stakeholders. Other focus areas are forging entirely new bodies of work or requiring a new lens on existing work. Making the case for why progress needs to be presented in a new way—even if that means stepping outside traditional reporting structures—can be achieved over time through early and ongoing engagement with partners.

Improving Connections

In reflecting on BJC's efforts to build the community health improvement strategy, several factors enable a systemwide approach. Some factors, such as BJC's governance structure, are already helping to create alignment. Others, like community health needs assessments (CHNAs) and the St. Louis Community Information Exchange (CIE), represent opportunities that can be further leveraged in the future.

Governance structures at multiple levels enable BJC to execute on the guiding principle of maintaining accountability to the communities it serves. Because community health improvement is a focus area for BJC, the work has greater visibility among the board and senior leadership. This facilitates integration with internal partners, including human resources; diversity, equity, and inclusion; supply chain; and patient experience teams (to name a few). In addition, each strategic focus area has a steering committee, with members representing various departments and facilities across BJC's system.

These committees then report to BJC's executive leadership. Each committee's knowledge and connections help guide the work, clear roadblocks, and expand community networks. In short, the approach to governance has been to leverage what exists to build stronger connections across the system. This model can be applied in other scenarios.

One example is the CHNAs that are completed every three years for each of BJC's 12 hospitals. These assessments offer data insights into community needs, and since 2016 have helped BJC build its muscle for collaborative action on community health priorities. BJC's community health improvement strategic plan was created with the understanding that each hospital identifies and commits to its own priorities through its CHNAs. The system efforts are not intended to replace the work outlined by hospital efforts; rather, BJC promotes complementary processes in which the system's priorities are informed by what is learned from staff on the front lines of local community health efforts, and their approach is informed by the capacities, resources, and partnerships the Community Health Improvement Team develops through its work.

The CIE is another way to create stronger system and region connections. Launched in 2020 in response to the COVID-19 pandemic, the CIE facilitates a regional coordinated entry system that connects client data across health and social service providers. With leadership and backbone support from the United Way of Greater St. Louis, the CIE and the broader Unite Missouri network connect partners through a shared technology platform that enables them to send and receive electronic referrals. BJC has been a lead partner in the development and implementation of this network and looks forward to understanding its impact, not only in terms of the extent to which it enhances BJC providers' understanding of patients' social needs and allows them to respond in real-time but also in facilitating more integrated social care systems across the region to address health equity.

CONCLUSION

To improve the health of our communities locally, regionally, and nationally, health systems must adopt the intentional change to move from what was and is to what could be. Addressing social standards for the delivery of care both inside and outside of hospital walls involves making a new or renewed commitment to community health improvement and taking the appropriate actions to address the root causes of health inequity, many of which include social conditions. BJC believes that all people can have an equal opportunity to live their healthiest lives. The vision requires that the institution change how it thinks about healthcare, move to a model that addresses the whole person, and affirm that social care is healthcare.

ACKNOWLEDGMENTS

The authors thank BJC HealthCare's Community Health Improvement Team leadership members Jason Q. Purnell, PhD, vice president of community health improvement; Karlos Bledsoe, Sr., director of strategy and operations; and Doneisha Bohannon, director of community health partnerships and collaboration, for their contributions. The authors also thank Rebeccah L. Bennett; Jessica Perkins; Natalie Parks, PhD; and Chelsey Carter, PhD, of Emerging Wisdom LLC, and Jacqueline Ferman-Grothe, director of media and public relations at BJC HealthCare.

REFERENCES

BJC HealthCare. 2021. "Community Health Improvement Strategic Plan 2022–2023." Emerging Wisdom. Published August. https://www.bjc.org/ community-health-improvement.

Braveman, P., and L. Gottlieb. 2014. "The Social Determinants of Health: It's Time to Consider the Cause of the Causes." *Public Health Reports 129* (1): 19–31. https://doi.org/10.1177/003335491412915206.

Cambria, N., P. Fehler, J. Q. Purnell, and B. Schmidt. 2018. "Segregation in St. Louis: Dismantling the Divide." St. Louis, MO: Washington University in St. Louis.

Gordon, C. 2008. *Mapping Decline: St. Louis and the Fate of the American City.* Philadelphia, PA: University of Pennsylvania Press.

Harper, S., R. F. MacLehose, and J. S. Kaufman. 2014. "Trends in the Black-White Life Expectancy Gap Among US States, 1990–2009." *Health Affairs 33* (8): 1375–82. https://doi.org/10.1377/hlthaff.2013.1273.

Holder, S., and D. Montgomery. 2019. "Life Expectancy Is Associated with Segregation in U.S. Cities." Bloomberg. Published June 6. https://www.bloomberg.com/news/articles/2019-06-06/life-expectancy-follows-segregation-in-u-scities.

King, C. J., B. O. Buckley, R. Maheshwari, and D. M. Griffith. 2022. "Race, Place, and Structural Racism: A Review of Health and History in Washington, D.C." *Health Affairs 41* (2): 273–80. https://doi.org/10.1377/hlthaff.2021.01805.

Kramer, M. R., and C. R. Hogue. 2009. "Is Segregation Bad for Your Health?" *Epidemiologic Reviews 31* (1): 178–94. https://doi.org/10.1093/epirev/ mxp001.

Purnell, J. Q., G. J. Camberos, and R. P. Fields (eds.). 2014. "For the Sake of All: A Report on the Health and Well-Being of African Americans in St. Louis and Why It Matters for Everyone." St. Louis, MO: Washington University in St. Louis and St. Louis University. https://cpb-us-w2.wpmucdn.com/ sites.wustl.edu/dist/3/1454/files/2018/06/ FSOA_report_2-17zd1xm.pdf.

Rothstein, R. 2014. "The Making of Ferguson: Public Policies at the Root of Its Troubles." Washington, DC: Economic Policy Institute. Published October 15. https://www.epi.org/publication/making-ferguson/.

Schroeder, S. A. 2007. "We Can Do Better—Improving the Health of the American People." *New England Journal of Medicine* 357 (12): 1221–8. https://doi.org/10.1056/NEJMsa073350.

FOR DISCUSSION

1. How does place matter in the quality of local healthcare delivery?
2. Who are potential partners in your service area? What services do they provide that you can leverage to serve local vulnerable populations?
3. BJC identified core roles that it can play with its partners and collaborators as it works to improve community health. How might these roles shift, and why?
4. How can a Community Information Exchange facilitate more equitable care delivery among partners?

Reimagining Healthcare to Meet Communities' Needs Outside Hospital Walls

RANDY OOSTRA, DM, FACHE

SUMMARY

Identifying and addressing the social determinants of health is an integral part of the mission at ProMedica as a health and well-being organization and an anchor institution in the communities we serve. For more than a decade, ProMedica has been on a progressive journey to integrate identification, screening, and interventions with important drivers of adverse outcomes to create a new model for healthcare, a model designed to bend the cost curve and enhance the health of our patients, clients, and communities. We are living our commitment to a healthier, thriving community by coupling high-quality care with community outreach and strategically implemented social care. Initiatives include job training, affordable housing initiatives, and financial coaching.

FOSTERING HEALTHY COMMUNITIES forms the core of Pro-Medica's mission, but the way to achieve that mission is evolving.

Clinical and medical care have been widely considered to be the determinants of health and well-being. At ProMedica, we were confidently serving patients within the walls of our hospitals and offices but then frequently sending them home into situations that were less than optimal for health—think food deserts, inadequate housing, and lack of access to follow-up care. In response, we launched the ProMedica National Social Determinants of Health Institute in 2018 and began investing in programs and research to address these inequities.

Studies show that 20 percent of health and well-being is determined by trips to our doctors and hospitals, while the remaining 80 percent relates to other factors such as the physical environment, social and economic factors, and health behaviors (Hood et al. 2016). As an organization, ProMedica is all-in on addressing the social determinants of health (SDOHs) and pulling together like-minded organizations for the effort.

TRANSFORMING A CARE DELIVERY MODEL

ProMedica began assessing SDOHs in early 2015 by conducting depression screens across its acute care and ambulatory settings. By 2016, we were using the Hunger Vital Sign screening tool for food insecurity as well (Hager et al. 2010). By 2017, we developed our own comprehensive screening that includes 10 domains and 24 clinically validated questions and implemented it across all our 48 primary care offices. We ask our patients to self-identify their social needs. The domains include food insecurity, housing, social connection, transportation, intimate partner violence, financial strain, childcare, education, job training and employment, and behavioral health.

To avoid disrupting the clinical flow, we began in January 2018 to provide patients with a tablet to complete the questionnaire in the office just before seeing their provider. This efficiency helped to increase completion rates. By July 2019, the screening tool was integrated into the patient portal so patients can complete the survey from home ahead of their visit date. Three out of four patients now complete the survey using that method, and our screening numbers have increased five-fold in two years.

Patients with identified needs are referred to the ProMedica Community Care Hub for further screening, support, and resource connection. The Hub is a group of social workers, nurses, and public health practitioners dedicated to helping patients find appropriate community support. The patients are classified by risk and, in some urgent cases, are referred to the Hub staff while they are still in the provider's office.

In comparison to our average patients, our Medicaid patients are nearly three times more likely to be at the high-risk rate for positive screens and seven times more likely to have an identified need in four or more domains. In our top 10 domains, Medicaid patients are also twice as likely to indicate issues related to food and housing insecurity and nearly twice as likely to cite educational and financial issues. Once a patient is connected with the Hub, the team works with them to address their needs. In a 20-month study of 2,150 Medicaid and non-Medicaid patients beginning in mid-2017, we determined that we were able to resolve issues in 68 percent of the cases.

Identifying Unmet Needs

ProMedica is streamlining and automating the identification of patients with unmet needs who are referred to the Hub or other services. This process is tracked within the electronic health record so our clinicians and care navigators can see what services patients were referred to and whether their needs were ultimately met by the Hub team and community partners.

Furthermore, we are using our wealth of screening, referral, and outcomes data to identify interventions that clearly move the needle on the triple aim of improving the experience and health of the patient while reducing the cost of care (the result of reduced admission, readmissions, and emergency department [ED] utilization) and improving connections to care continuity. Achieving cost reduction for patients has enabled us to secure funding from health plans for interventions such as financial coaching and food clinic visits. As we continue to identify interventions that make a measurable impact on health outcomes and costs, we partner with other institutions to scale these programs for more patients and community residents.

HEALTHY FOODS, HEALTHY LIVES

Since ProMedica's concentration on hunger as a health issue began in 2014, we have screened nearly 5 million patients for food insecurity and have embedded food security into our care delivery model. Our screenings have revealed that a high percentage of people are motivated to change various social factors that harm their health but lack the ability or knowledge to do so.

To connect more patients with food resources in a convenient way, ProMedica opened its first on-site food clinic in 2015. Individuals who receive care from a ProMedica physician or clinic and indicate that they struggle to afford sufficient food every month are given a referral to the clinic and may visit it monthly over a six-month period. (Referrals may be renewed with a visit to a ProMedica primary care physician and another positive food insecurity screening.) Dieticians at the clinic provide individualized nutrition counseling and guide patients to the best food choices for their health conditions (e.g., diabetes and obesity). ProMedica now operates three food clinics and regularly evaluates the impact of food clinic use on patient health. A June 2021 evaluation conducted by social risk analytics firm Socially Determined found that the food clinic has played an effective role in reducing suboptimal use of healthcare services and has reduced ED visits. When compared to a control group of patients with a similar health profile, patients who visited the food clinic visited the ED at a rate 1.7 times lower than patients who made no visits to the clinic.

In 2020, ProMedica expanded its food insecurity commitment by launching ProMedica Farms and Veggie Mobile van at Pro-Medica Charles and Virginia Hickman Hospital, just across the state border in Lenawee County, Michigan. This initiative provides youth educational programs, employee volunteering, therapeutic quiet space for hospital patients and staff, and freshly grown food to the community.

ProMedica continues to design and test new programs to meet patients' nonclinical needs. In 2022, we received the USDA's Gus Schumacher Nutrition Incentive Program Award, which will enable us to fill produce prescriptions that food-insecure pregnant patients can redeem at grocery stores for 12 months. We will evaluate the impact of this initiative on the health outcomes of both pregnant patient and child.

FINANCIAL WELLNESS NETWORK

Recognizing that financial strain is often at the heart of many other social needs for its patients, ProMedica launched a financial coaching program in 2016. Today, the ProMedica Financial Wellness Network (FWN) provides financial education and personalized counseling for hundreds of community members. FWN also offers a digital literacy series to improve computer skills and market-ability to prospective employers. Two ProMedica centers in rural Ohio provide services to low- and moderate-income families such as securing living-wage jobs, building credit, reducing debt, and gaining financial security.

SDOH interventions include face-to-face and virtual career and financial coaching to build good money management habits. This no-cost service has helped participants boost credit scores by an average of 42 points, increase net income by $894, and reduce their average debt by more than $6,000.

INVESTMENTS IN NEW LIFE

Launched in 2018 as part of ProMedica's community anchor mission strategy, the ProMedica Ebeid Neighborhood Promise (ENP, named after local philanthropist Russell J. Ebeid) is a catalytic, multifaceted initiative developed to address SDOHs and create a model to revitalize neighborhoods. ProMedica launched the ENP model with a $50 million investment in long-term neighborhood health and growth in Toledo's UpTown. This historically disinvested and economically distressed neighborhood is adjacent to the city's downtown where ProMedica relocated its headquarters operations in 2017. The ENP effort in UpTown tackles four urgent concerns: improving health outcomes, increasing access to education, offering job training, and providing stable housing.

The ProMedica Ebeid Center puts promise into practice. To make the connection between dietary health and community health, the Ebeid Center is the home of Market on the Green, an affordable healthy grocery store in the former food desert. Three additional floors provide classrooms for nursing aide training, cooking classes, financial coaching services, and additional educational opportunities.

To build on the momentum of the Ebeid Center, ProMedica recently partnered with Bitwise Industries, a tech apprenticeship engine, to launch the Jefferson Center in 2023. This wealth-building innovation center will accelerate partnerships with entrepreneurs and businesses, support workforce development, and facilitate technology. Racial, ethnic, socioeconomic, and gender diversity will be at the core of the Jefferson Center mission. The apprenticeship approach allows people to earn while they learn, thus removing the financial barriers of traditional education and professional advancement opportunities to high-wage, high-growth jobs.

Building on its local successes, the ENP is expanding into Adrian, Michigan, where ProMedica has partnered with the Lenawee Community Foundation and All About Adrian Resident Coalition to deploy a development program for the marginalized rural community. ProMedica has committed a $20 million place-based investment to the project and is working with the local organizations to identify plans that will yield the best financial—and social—returns for the community.

THE IMPACT FUND

ProMedica is committed not only to incorporating SDOH interventions into its care delivery model and community investment strategy but also to leading the healthcare sector at large in evolving a care delivery model for better health. In 2020, ProMedica doubled down on this commitment by launching the Impact Fund, which supports the work of its Social Determinants of Health Institute in scaling and measuring the impact of promising programs, advocating for critical governmental policy changes, and enabling other healthcare institutions to replicate proven programs.

Healthy Homes for Healthy People

ProMedica is partnering with the Green & Healthy Homes Initiative (GHHI) to expand the nonprofit's whole-home model. The GHHI addresses health and racial equity by improving the health, safety, and energy efficiency of existing homes, typically leveraging public and private funds to maximize impact (www.greenandhealthyhomes. org). ProMedica has recognized the clear relationship between the health of a home and the health of its residents and joined forces with the GHHI to improve at least 7,000 homes over three years in several cities. ProMedica's goal is not only to make a direct positive impact on the lives of the residents in each of these homes but also to make the case that an investment in healthy home rehabilitation generates a positive social return.

THE NEEDS OF EMPLOYEES

ProMedica also supports its employees' well-being as part of its social commitment. In the wake of the COVID-19 pandemic and amid widespread economic pressures, employee needs are connected to social and economic factors more closely than ever. Healthcare leaders can and should play a role in improving the health and well-being of their employees.

Most employers offer health insurance coverage and sponsor a variety of well-being programs. These benefits are critical, yet they form only a piece of the total health puzzle. Employees who are struggling with putting food on the table or having a difficult time making it to work because of transportation and childcare challenges can have a direct and negative impact on their employer's business. These employees are understandably less engaged and productive at work and may have health conditions that are being improperly managed, which increases the overall cost of care.

In dollar terms, absenteeism and lower productivity tied to financial stress cost an estimated $2,412 per year, per employee (Francolini 2022). Employees can be happier, more productive, and more satisfied when they are engaged and feel like their employer cares about them as a person. Since 2021, more than 3,000 employees of several companies, including ProMedica, have completed a confidential SDOH assessment using Resourceful, a tool developed by ProMedica and the well-being consultant Kumanu. The assessment spans a wide range of industries and pay scales, yet several common challenges have risen to the top: food insecurity, financial strain, and behavioral (mental) health. At ProMedica, we are now identifying and connecting employees with resources and using aggregate data to inform the development of new employee benefits and wellness programs.

CONCLUSION

ProMedica has more than 10 years of experience in addressing SDOHs, and yet we are only getting started as we look beyond the clinical model of healthcare that is delivered within the walls of the hospital. As we expand that traditional view to include social factors, we find more healthful benefits to the community—including our employees. Developing, scaling, and advocating for solutions centered in SDOHs can lead to new ways to improve the health and well-being of whole communities.

At a time when people face mounting stressors in their lives at home and at work, more healthcare leaders will be wise to take the lead in their communities and screen for SDOHs, and then take appropriate interventions. When that happens, there can be a radical redirection toward a healthier world.

REFERENCES

Francolini, S. 2022. "Another Rising Cost for Employers: Financial Stress." John Hancock. Published February 15, 2022. https://retirement.johnhancock.com/us/en/viewpoints/financialwellness/another-rising-cost-for-employers–financial-stress.

Hager, E. R., A. M. Quigg, M. M. Black, S. M. Coleman, T. Heeren, R. Rose-Jacobs, J. T. Cook, S. A. Ettinger de Cuba, P. H. Casey, M. Chilton, D. B. Cutts, A. F. Meyers, and D. A. Frank. 2010. "Development and Validity of a 2-Item Screen to Identify Families at Risk for Food Insecurity." *Pediatrics* 126 (1): e26–e32. https://doi.org/10. 1542/peds.2009-3146.

Hood, C. M., K. P. Gennuso, G. R. Swain, and B. B. Catlin. 2016. "County Health Rankings: Relationships Between Determinant Factors and Health Outcomes." *American Journal of Preventive Medicine 50* (2): 129–35. https://doi.org/10.1016/j.amepre.2015.08.024.

FOR DISCUSSION

1. What are some commonly identified social determinants of health that are possible inflection points to improve health equity?
2. What tactics can healthcare providers take to improve their communities' health in multifaceted ways that are unrelated to clinical care?
3. How can insurance coverage and wellness programs be enhanced to support employees? In the context of ESG, why are such investments worthwhile?

Reverse Ride-Alongs Connect Medical Caregivers with Their Community

JANICE G. MURPHY, MSN, FACHE

SUMMARY

Many police departments have ride-along programs in which community residents accompany police officers in the field. Community organizers in one Cleveland, Ohio, neighborhood took that concept and flipped it to create a "reverse ride-along" program. During a reverse ride-along, police officers take part in community tours and dialogues to learn more about the area they serve and explore issues involving trust and trauma. In 2019, the reverse ride-along program added medical care providers from St. Vincent Charity Medical Center. The program was designed to connect residents and medical professionals for conversations in which learned knowledge and lived knowledge are valued equally. Participants identify barriers that deter positive health outcomes and prohibit effective engagement with the medical system. They do that by defining the social constructs unique to the community, then developing opportunities to address the barriers.

FOR MANY YEARS, police departments across the United States have offered ride-along programs in which community residents accompany police officers in the field to gain a better understanding of their work. Community organizers in Cleveland's Central neighborhood have taken that concept and flipped it by creating a "reverse ride-along" program.

During a reverse ride-along, police officers participate in community tours and dialogue with local residents to learn more about the people, places, and resources in the area they serve. Together, the police officers and residents explore issues involving trust and trauma.

In 2019, the Cleveland program, which is coordinated by the community organizations that created it—Cleveland Central Promise Neighborhood, Inner Visions Cleveland, Neighborhood Connections, and Another Chance of Ohio—added medical care providers from St. Vincent Charity Medical Center, a Catholic hospital in the Central neighborhood. Throughout its long history, St. Vincent Charity has routinely engaged in outreach with local residents and institutions. The goal of this reverse ride-along is to gather a firsthand appreciation of the community's assets and an understanding of its social needs. This article describes reverse ride-alongs as experienced by doctors from St. Vincent Charity's graduate medical education (GME) program.

THE CENTRAL NEIGHBORHOOD STORY

Central is located immediately southeast of Cleveland's central business district and is bisected by Central Avenue. Beginning in the 1930s, several public housing projects were constructed in Central, and they significantly altered the landscape of retail shops that served a poor, primarily European population. Displaced by the new construction, that population was able to muster the resources to move out, leaving behind a poor, less mobile Black population that has become dependent on Medicaid insurance and social services.

A NETWORK OF TRUST AND COLLABORATION

The reverse ride-along program was initially intent on build-ing networks of trust and collaboration between social services providers and their constituents. The theoretical underpinning was that increased knowledge of a community's assets can lead to improved service delivery and outcomes. As applied to the healthcare sector, the reverse ride-along connects residents and medical professionals on an even playing field where learned and lived knowledge are valued equally. Everyone involved is provided the opportunity to identify the barriers that deter posi-tive health outcomes and prohibit effective engagement with the medical system.

A quote from one of the St. Vincent Charity GME participants, shared in a survey, clearly states the need for the reverse ride-along program: "I really don't know what this community is like, even though every day I see patients who live here."

As Joseph Black, program officer for health equity at Sisters of Charity Foundation of Cleveland and an organizer of the reverse ride-along program, explained in a recent personal communication with the author, "We bring service providers into the community to interact with and to build relationships in a non-threatening situation in which people organically get to know each other. What is the benefit of knowing a doctor who knows the community? It creates a foundation for us to better understand each other. Our focus is to treat each other as people, stripping down titles so we can see each other as humans."

The unequal title-driven power dynamic is pervasive in minority and low-income communities, which is why organizers of the reverse ride-along connect community residents and medical profession-als. In this shared space, all can build relationships that can lead to solutions to serve the best interests of everyone and inform best practices for improved health outcomes.

THE JOURNEY TO UNDERSTANDING

Because many of the students in the GME program are not from Cleveland and had limited knowledge of the Central community, the typical four-hour itinerary includes two stops for dialogue with residents. The following sections recap the experiences in one recent reverse ride-along.

Touring the Central Community

The tour highlighted assets such as local community leaders, religious institutions, schools, medical facilities, social service agencies, and more. Throughout the experience, the medical care providers learned how health outcomes were being affected by public housing accommodations, inconvenient food access, trauma (i.e., bearing witness to violent crime or being otherwise affected by it), mass incarceration, and local schools.

Eating and Sharing

Cornucopia Place

Serving food is a best practice when coordinating community conversations. In reverse ride-alongs, participants share a meal from Sunshine Café, a restaurant with healthy food options. The cafe is inside Cornucopia Place, a facility that provides nutrition education, cooking demonstrations, and a harvest preparation station for local gardeners. Over lunch, the reverse ride-along group discussed access to health resources and information in the Central neighborhood. They covered healthcare concerns such as:

- What is your understanding of the community's access to health resources?

- How is this information shared in the community and in hospitals?
- What can residents and medical professionals do to improve people's access to vital resources and information?

The discussions brought several themes to light:

- Residents said that they had to leave the community to get fresh food and produce.
- Residents expressed the desire for healthcare facilities in the community.
- St. Vincent Charity, while known as a supportive environment for patients dealing with mental distress, was underused because of the stigma attached to behavioral healthcare and the lack of child and adolescent health services.

Friendly Inn Settlement House

A pillar of the neighborhood, Friendly Inn Settlement House has served Central for more than 145 years. Programs include an early childhood enrichment center, individual and family support programs, after-school youth programs, and a food bank. At Friendly Inn, the ride-along participants divided into small groups to discuss two crucial topics: the impact of trauma on the community and the relationship between medical institutions and the community.

The GME students wanted to understand the impact of trauma on the personal and professional lives of the residents. They wanted to know what they could do to help. The following key discussion themes surfaced:

- Residents value being able to connect with medical professionals on a personal level.
- Residents want to be informed and included in decisions about their health.

- Residents are distrustful of medical professionals because of the historical mistreatment of Blacks in the United States and a perceived lack of understanding of their concerns.
- Medical professionals get burned out when caring for distrustful chronically ill patients who do not heed their advice.
- Residents are traumatized by the violent crime and extreme poverty that surround them.
- The search to find healthy, affordable food is a constant struggle.
- Residents nevertheless remain resilient and appreciate the positive attributes of life in their neighborhood such as its strong sense of history, mutual support, and creative problem-solving.

Given the evident stressors, how can the community and medical institutions work together to understand each other better? This question prompted the following discussion points:

- Hospitals gain benefits from encouraging medical professionals to go out in the community because they can develop a better understanding of local barriers to care, which, in turn, can help them make better-informed treatment decisions for their patients and keep them out of emergency departments.
- Medical professionals should explore the whole picture of the people they serve, which requires a full understanding of the community and its resources.
- Residents want to see that medical professionals truly want the health of residents to improve.
- Residents want medical professionals to get to know them on a personal level and build genuinely personable relationships.

- Residents face barriers to making appointments with medical professionals such as office hours that conflict with work and school schedules and a lack of transportation.
- When selecting a care provider, parents of young children need a site that is convenient in terms of both hours and location.
- Word of mouth is the most effective form of advertisement for a hospital.

The connection between trauma and the lack of mutual understanding became evident in the dialogue at Friendly Inn. Many Central residents said that they do not partake in preventative healthcare. On the occasions when they do need to visit a doctor, they explained, they typically experience information overload and confusion. Doctors speak over them or do not clearly explain how they are supposed to take medication or why certain tests or follow-up care is being prescribed. And if they go for an examination or to see about something minor and then leave with a frightening diagnosis, they will avoid going back.

During the discussion, one of the ride-along GME students offered the physician's perspective on this communication issue: "Medical practitioners are often aware they may not see this patient again for a while, or ever, and so they feel an urgency to provide as much information as possible. We are trying to help as much as we can in the limited time we have, but I understand that it can be scary and overwhelming. Starting the visit with a conversation about goals and finding a common goal between doctor and patient seems like a good way to build trust."

Closing Activity

At the beginning of the facilitated session, each participant was given a piece of paper and asked to write a statement that identified them by a role they played (mother, nurse, friend, public servant) and what they saw as their greatest strength. At the close of the session, each was asked to write on the opposite side of that paper what they learned in the reverse ride-along. Then, all pieces of paper were linked with tape. This chain symbolized a new community where individual roles and strengths can be united to forge a common bond that helps people recognize each other's special worth.

REVERSE RIDE-ALONG RESULTS

As highlighted in the reverse ride-along described in this article, the primary result is a better mutual understanding between medical care providers and the people in the communities they serve.

St. Vincent Charity participants in reverse ride-along events report improved relationships, increased trust, and better collaboration to identify appropriate solutions. Those solutions include better access to healthcare, food, affordable and safe housing, education opportunities, employment, arts and recreation options, and transportation.

Also, in response to participation in the reverse ride-along program, St. Vincent Charity has established new social initiatives to increase the frequency and depth of connections among caregivers and residents. These include a hospital community advisory board, which brings stakeholders together quarterly via Zoom to unpack the social themes raised by residents and increase trust. These meetings facilitate conversations to confirm the accuracy of knowledge and determine the best paths forward together as St. Vincent Charity continues to provide outpatient services in behavioral health, addiction treatment, and primary care.

CONCLUSION

Connecting community residents and medical professionals in a space where all participants are equal builds supportive relationships and leads to solutions that benefit all parties. The key applications to the practice of reverse ride-alongs include

- organizing community leaders and residents to directly engage with their medical professionals;
- determining how best to organize and tailor each ride-along to cover what is most important for medical professionals to know based on their care specialties;
- allowing the program to be led by residents who can identify the assets in their communities; and
- ensuring that medical professionals are guided by the question, "How can we engage with residents to discuss health from the community's perspective?"

The reverse ride-alongs have helped the Sisters of Charity Health System's St. Vincent Charity Medical Center more fully engage with its community by integrating the voice of the residents into the creation of effective services and partnerships. This social strategy includes working to translate the community's ideas into physical spaces and programmatic clusters to span an inclusive broad notion of health across body, mind, and spirit.

ACKNOWLEDGMENTS

The reverse ride-along project with St. Vincent Charity Medical Center was coordinated by Joseph Black of the Sisters of Charity Foundation of Cleveland and Cleveland Central Promise Neighborhood, Jan Thrope of Inner Visions of Cleveland, Jerry Pena of Neighborhood Connections, and Barbara Anderson of Another Chance of Ohio. The reverse ride-alongs with GME students are supported by funding from the Better Health Partnership.

FOR DISCUSSION

1. How could a reverse ride-along address issues of trust/mistrust and trauma?
2. What are some of the program takeaways for St. Vincent Charity participants?
3. When a title-driven power dynamic is pervasive in minority and low-income communities, how can doctors and patients both be harmed?
4. How well do you know your community? What are its greatest needs?

Governance

Sustainable Healthcare Depends on Good Governance Practices

RICHARD G. GREENHILL, DHA, FACHE, AND MERETTE KHALIL

SUMMARY

Effective leadership and governance are at the heart of creating and maintaining resilient health systems. COVID-19 exposed a plethora of issues in its wake, most notably the need to plan for resilience. Facing threats that swirl around climate, fiscal solvency, and emerging infectious diseases, healthcare leaders are challenged to think broadly on issues that affect operational viability. The global healthcare community has offered numerous approaches, frameworks, and criteria to assist leaders in creating strategies for better health governance, security, and resilience. As the world exits the worst of the pandemic, now is the time to plan for the sustainability of those strategies. Based on guidance developed by the World Health Organization, good governance is one key to sustainability. Healthcare leaders who develop measures to assess and monitor progress toward strengthening resilience can achieve sustainable development goals.

GOVERNANCE DESCRIBES THE mechanisms that organizations use to achieve their goals, both strategic and operational. The term is conceptual and hard to define, but the results of effective governance are tangible. In healthcare delivery, the emphasis has long been on operations and service provision. Today, however, healthcare systems and providers must also consider sustainability and resilience in the complex mix of measures that determine overall success.

COVID-19 and other world events over the past 5–10 years have reshaped what it means to be sustainable in healthcare. Before the onset of the pandemic in 2020, inequities in health were rampant and frequently resulted in the marginalization of the world's most vulnerable people. During the pandemic, the global health apparatus underwent the most significant stress test of operational capacity, resilience, and governance in recent memory. Most healthcare systems felt the pressure but did not have measures to quantify the complete impact. Now, as the world learns to function with COVID-19 and its variants, attention must shift to resilience as a component of effective governance.

HEALTH GOVERNANCE AND RESILIENCE

In the discussion of environmental, social, and governance (ESG) criteria, governance includes all factors that influence leadership activities, from board composition to succession planning, as well as pay for executives. Effective governance can ensure health security, health equity, and corporate resilience in the face of emergencies and pandemic preparedness.

In recent years, initiatives have been put forth to promote the role of governance across the healthcare continuum. These include

- the Global Health Security Agenda (GHSA; https:// globalhealthsecurityagenda.org/),
- International Health Regulations (IHRs; www.who.int /health-topics/international-health-regulations), and

- Sustainable Development Goals (SDGs; https://sdgs.un
  .org/goals).

These initiatives emphasize resilience and sustainability in the practices of care delivery.

The movement toward more sustainable care has yielded exemplars across the United States. Each year, Practice Greenhealth announces winners of its awards for sustainability in a host of areas. Several examples of organizations that are effectively aligning strategic goals with environmentally sustainable efforts toward resilience are listed in Exhibit 1, which describes each organization and its approach. Each is marked according to its contribution toward pollution reduction, energy conservation, and environmental protection.

As shown in Exhibit 1, integration of the SDGs into strategic frameworks is an approach toward a more resilient and sustainable system. The United Nations Sustainable Development Agenda for 2030 includes national strategy goals for countries across the globe to enhance sustainability. The primary SDGs (and their targets) that are closely aligned with health system sustainability include SDG 3 (targets 3.4, 3.8), 10 (10.3, 10.4), and 11 (11.5).

Exhibit 1: Examples of Sustainable Efforts in US Healthcare Delivery

Organization	Description	Pollution Reduction	Energy Resilience	Environmental Sustainability
Abraham Lincoln Memorial Hospital	Reduction of 80% of anesthetic gas purchase	X		X
Boston Medical Center	Cogeneration power plant		X	
Cleveland Clinic	30% of local food sourcing			X

Exhibit 1: Examples of Sustainable Efforts in US Healthcare Delivery *(continued)*

Organization	Description	Pollution Reduction	Energy Resilience	Environmental Sustainability
Hackensack Meridian Health– Hackensack University Medical Center	Sustainable food purchasing	X		X
Hackensack Meridian Health– Jersey Shore University Medical Center	Reduction in mean use in patient meals	X		X
Hudson Hospital (HealthPartners)	Use of "veggie prescriptions" to improve access			X
Lakeview Hospital (HealthPartners)	Use of sustainability councils	X	X	X
Memorial Sloan-Kettering Cancer Center	Use of sustainability task forces	X	X	X
Overlook Medical Center (Atlantic Health)	Reduction of surgical blue wrap	X		X

Exhibit 1: Examples of Sustainable Efforts in US Healthcare Delivery *(continued)*

Organization	Description	Pollution Reduction	Energy Resilience	Environmental Sustainability
Ronald Reagan UCLA Medical Center	All-electric buses for patient and staff transport	X	X	X
Stony Brook University Hospital	Green space design	X	X	X
VHA Erie VA Medical Center	Reduced water consumption			X

Source: Adapted from Practice Greenhealth. https://practicegreenhealth.org/data-and-awards/awards-and-recognition.

SDG 3: Good Health and Well-Being

- **Target 3.4.** Reduce by one-third premature mortality from noncommunicable diseases (NCDs) through prevention and treatment and promote mental health and well-being.
- **Target 3.8.** Provide universal health coverage including financial risk protection; access to quality essential healthcare services; and access to safe, effective, and affordable essential medicines and vaccines for all.

SDG 10: Reduced Inequalities

- Target 10.3: Ensure equal opportunity and reduce inequalities of outcomes by eliminating discriminatory laws, policies, and practices and promoting appropriate legislation and policies.

- Target 10.4: Adopt policies—especially fiscal, wage, and social protection policies—and progressively improve equality.

SDG 11: Sustainable Cities and Communities

- Target 11.5: Significantly reduce deaths from disasters and substantially decrease the direct economic losses caused by disasters, especially losses felt by the poor and vulnerable.

How is *health governance* defined and implemented? How is progress measured? Exhibit 1 includes real-world examples that healthcare governing bodies might consider for establishing and measuring tangible goals. Initially, it might be prudent for healthcare leaders to understand baselines so they can determine how their organization contributes to pollution and consumes energy, and then more fully appreciate its impact on the local environment. These three targets (pollution reduction, energy resilience, environmental sustainability) collectively represent a great starting point to create governance goals and objectives to assess operational influences and their associated impact on health in the local communities. This is not a simple undertaking, but the baselines yield important benchmarks for improvement.

GOVERNANCE AND EQUITY IN CARE

Many healthcare organizations have made strides in dealing with inequity in their systems. The Institute for Healthcare Improvement (www.ihi.org/Topics/Health-Equity), American Medical Association (www.ama-assn.org/about/ama-center-health-equity), and American Hospital Association (https://equity.aha.org/) are just a few that have put forth initiatives to address the inequitable delivery of care. However, building sustainability into health equity requires a deep dive into causes beyond superficial anecdotes. Sustainable health equity can be cultivated through data-driven and measurable actions that are reinforced with good governance at the board and C-suite levels. An example is Healthfirst, a nonprofit insurer in New York. The company leverages technology and incentives for providers to serve vulnerable communities through principles in its ADVANCE framework for equity outlined in Exhibit 2.

Exhibit 2: Healthfirst ADVANCE Equity Principles

Available to all people, with equal opportunity to access quality care.

Data-informed to close gaps in care and support care continuity and coordination.

Value-driven through hospital, physician, and insurer alignment around optimal care.

Accessible when and where help is needed, so everyone is surrounded with opportunities for healthcare access and continuous insurance with no gaps.

Nurturing and human-centered so it's easy to engage and navigate.

Community-based with strong ties to services and resources that promote whole-person care and address social determinants of health.

Evidence-based with the best available clinical expertise and research guiding every treatment plan, care decision, and public-health intervention.

Source: Adapted from Healthfirst Advance (2023). https://advance.healthfirst .org/.

The payer aims to close coverage gaps for its 1.7 million members who speak 70 different languages. Guiding principles in the ADVANCE framework demonstrate organizational commitment to equity, which directly aligns with SDG targets 10.3 and 10.4 as well as the quintuple aim of improving population health, enhancing the care experience, reducing costs, supporting caregivers' well-being, and advancing health equity.

POPULATION HEALTH MANAGEMENT

In considering governance under ESG, healthcare boards should support sustainable health practices in their local populations. The rationale behind the SDG 2030 Agenda is to shift the world population onto a sustainable and resilient path. Thus, healthcare providers must look beyond care delivery and integrate their efforts with community partners to be most effective. Many healthcare organizations have approached population health as a rebrand of the measures already being tracked that are tied to reimbursement, such as readmissions. However, effective management of population health extends beyond the *event* of a readmission and gets to the *underlying causes* of that readmission. Governance strategies should measure and intervene in those areas to make measurable improvements, as indicated in SDG 3.4 for NCDs.

The target for SDG 3.4 is critical to well-being related to the associated financial burden of NCDs and their morbidity. Likewise, SDG target 3.8 relates to achieving essential health services coverage to reduce financial burden and risk to patients. The Organisation for Economic Co-operation and Development (2019) notes that success with the SDGs relies on the tactical use of budgetary, procurement, and regulatory tools, along with the strategic design and implementation of innovative policies and programs. Tactical examples can be found in programs like those administered through Medicaid as well as Health Resources and Services Administration grants.

Exhibit 3: Governance in PHM for Achieving SDG 3.4 and SDG 3.8

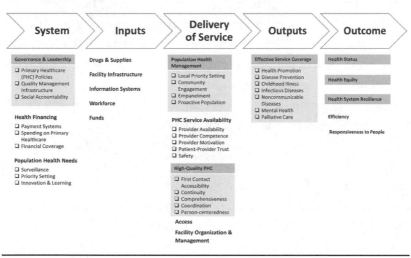

System ▷ Inputs ▷ Delivery of Service ▷ Outputs ▷ Outcome

Governance & Leadership	Drugs & Supplies	Population Health Management	Effective Service Coverage	Health Status
❑ Primary Healthcare (PHC) Policies	Facility Infrastructure	❑ Local Priority Setting	❑ Health Promotion	
❑ Quality Management Infrastructure	Information Systems	❑ Community Engagement	❑ Disease Prevention	Health Equity
❑ Social Accountability	Workforce	❑ Empanelment	❑ Childhood Illness	
		❑ Proactive Population	❑ Infectious Diseases	Health System Resilience
	Funds		❑ Noncommunicable Diseases	
Health Financing		PHC Service Availability	❑ Mental Health	Efficiency
❑ Payment Systems		❑ Provider Availability	❑ Palliative Care	
❑ Spending on Primary Healthcare		❑ Provider Competence		Responsiveness to People
❑ Financial Coverage		❑ Provider Motivation		
		❑ Patient-Provider Trust		
Population Health Needs		❑ Safety		
❑ Surveillance		High-Quality PHC		
❑ Priority Setting		❑ First Contact Accessibility		
❑ Innovation & Learning		❑ Continuity		
		❑ Comprehensiveness		
		❑ Coordination		
		❑ Person-centeredness		
		Access		
		Facility Organization & Management		

Source: Adapted from Primary Health Care Performance Initiative (2018). https://improvingphc.org/.

Population health management (PHM) is important in facilitating progress toward targets SDG 3.4 and 3.8. PHM programs are centered on curative as well as preventive health, NCD management for improved quality of life, and healthcare provision improvements that reduce costs. Exhibit 3 illustrates the process of governance as an enabler in the healthcare system leading to desirable outcomes in care delivery.

PHM supports proactive primary healthcare in accordance with the Medicare Access and CHIP Reauthorization Act of 2015 (MACRA) and value-based care. Deloitte's 2017 survey of US hospital CEOs validated the crucial role of PHM in value-based care payment models (Burrill and Kane 2017). In the absence of universal health coverage in the United States, value-based care models can be applied to PHM in tackling waste and reducing costs through the integration of chronic disease management and improved access to care (Zieff et al. 2020). While waste reduction is associated with organizational and fiscal sustainability, it does little to directly address the true causes of health disparities and health inequity in population health. The US Department of Health and Human Services has initiated the Healthy People PHM program to target NCDs' modifiable determinants (https://health.gov/healthypeople). The prevention of risk before the commencement of irreversible complications is an important goal of the program.

Dynamic technology supports successful and sustainable PHM. For example, Grand View Research has created an array of services for PHM and ESG activities. Its PHM open application programming interface can be used to manage NCD conditions to reduce the cost of care (Grand View Research n.d.). The PHM software facilitates the analysis of patient data to support decision-making and improve patient outcomes. In the post-COVID-19 pandemic era, top PHM service providers will be able to transform the PHM landscape in the United States using advanced technologies and data science. This will generate the data to track progress in achieving SDGs such as reduction in premature deaths from NCDs (SDG 3.4) and access to essential health services and financial risk protection (SDG 3.8).

As a multinational example, the European endeavor called EURO-HEALTHY used a scenario-driven approach to identify and track intercontinental drivers of population health inequities (Alvarenga et al. 2019). The project put forth three scenarios—(1) worst case, (2) to the best of our knowledge, and (3) best case—to identify factors present and expected to affect Europe regarding PHM inequities through 2030. The result of this is a population health index to inform policy decisions toward meeting the 2030 SDG Agenda.

While this project spanned several healthcare, political, and social systems that differ from US systems, there are some relatable governance nuggets. For example, EURO-HEALTHY found 176 drivers of inequities across political, environmental, social, technological, legal, and environmental domains. In each domain, the drivers were ranked to enable prioritization of resources and energy for the things that a healthcare system can influence (and identify those that are out of scope). These driver configurations could easily serve as a basis for governance in PHM sustainability, particularly around inequity. The sustainability of PHM in the US systems of care must involve policymakers (government level) and healthcare leadership champions (health system level), along with community involvement at the local and regional levels.

HEALTH SYSTEM SUSTAINABILITY

Resilience in healthcare has mostly been viewed in governance from a fiscal standpoint, with more recent consideration of environmental sustainability and health equity. A more comprehensive approach to governance might evolve through the understanding of hospital resilience core capacities codified by Khalil and colleagues (2022):

Exhibit 4: Areas of Focus for Hard and Soft Resilience in Hospitals

Hard Resilience	Soft Resilience
Space includes infrastructure and space utilization agility.	Systems and strategies includes planning, adaptive leadership, and management.
	Staff includes the clinicians and nonclinicians who do the day-to-day work.
	Stuff includes supply chain mechanisms, finance, and logistical operations.

Source: Adapted from Khalil et al. (2022).

absorption, adaptation, transformation, and learning. Hospitals' resilience is ultimately intertwined with the resilience of the overall health system and the communities they serve. Within this conceptual framework, strengthened hospital resilience requires both hard and soft qualities, as illustrated in Exhibit 4.

This approach fortifies the pillars of governance and equity in healthcare to support people, places, and planet. The ultimate outcome is sustainable economic, human, and social development.

CONCLUSION

The challenges to creating and maintaining sustainability depend on ESG factors related to health equity in care delivery, sustainable development, and resilience. In the movement to build sustainability in the US system, healthcare governing bodies should keep the following points at the forefront of their perspectives:

- Health is more than what occurs in the walls of healthcare providers; it includes environmental and social determinants.
- Inequities in the provision of care are costly and deadly.
- Health systems function in communities, and they must be full partners with others in providing care to the populations they serve.

When organizations fully understand their impact on their local environments, they can then create governance structures to cultivate sustainability and resilience. Empowered by that understanding, healthcare leaders can make evidence-based policy decisions. With equity and inclusion integrated into the approach, the system can work for everyone.

ACKNOWLEDGMENTS

Hamid Ravaghi, PhD, regional adviser at the World Health Organization Eastern Mediterranean Regional Office in Cairo, Egypt, and Tosin Dotun-Olujinmi, DHA, public health scientist at IDEY Public Health Consulting Inc., in Ottawa, Canada, contributed to this article.

REFERENCES

Alvarenga, A., C. A. Bana e Costa, C. Borrell, P. Lopes Ferreira, Â. Freitas, L. Freitas, M. D. Oliveira, T. C. Rodrigues, P. Santana, M. Lopes Santos, and A. C. L. Vieira. 2019. "Scenarios for Population Health Inequalities in 2030 in Europe: The EURO-HEALTHY Project Experience." *International Journal for Equity in Health* 18 (1): 100. https://doi.org/10.1186/s12939-019-1000-8.

Burrill, S., and A. Kane. 2017. "Population Health and Value-Based Care: Hospital CEO Survey Series." In *Deloitte 2017 Survey of US Health System CEOs: Moving Forward in an Uncertain Environment.* www2.deloitte.com/us/en/pages/lifesciences-and-health-care/articles/populationhealth-based-model.html.

Grand View Research. n.d. "U.S. Population Health Management Market Size, Share & Trends Analysis Report by Product (Software, Services), By End Use (Providers, Payers, Employer Groups), and Segment Forecasts, 2022–2030 (Report Overview)." Accessed October 28, 2022. www.grandviewresearch.com/industry-analysis/us-population-health-managementmarket.

Khalil, M., H. Ravaghi, D. Samhouri, J. Abo, A. Ali, H. Sakr, and A. Camacho. 2022. "What Is 'Hospital Resilience'? A Scoping Review on Conceptualization, Operationalization, and

Evaluation." *Frontiers in Public Health* 10: 1009400. https://
doi.org/10.3389/fpubh.2022.1009400.

Organisation for Economic Co-operation and Development.
2019. "Highlights. Governance as an SDG Accelerator: Country Experiences and Tools." Published July 16. www.oecd.org
/publications/governance-as-an-sdg-accelerator0666b085-en
.htm.

Zieff, G., Z. Y. Kerr, J. B. Moore, and L. Stoner. 2020. "Universal Healthcare in the United States of America: A Healthy
Debate." *Medicina* 56 (11): 580. https://doi.org/10.3390
/medicina56110580.

FOR DISCUSSION

1. In the discussion of environmental, social, and
   governance (ESG) criteria, what does governance
   comprise?
2. How can a healthcare governing body take an active
   role in pollution reduction, energy resilience, and
   environmental sustainability?
3. The UN's Sustainable Development Agenda includes
   goals and targets for organizational resilience. Describe a
   goal and one of its targets in healthcare.
4. How can value-based care models be applied to public
   health management in tackling waste and reducing
   costs?

Aligning Healthcare's Mission with Corporate Social Responsibility Action

MICHAEL J. DOWLING

SUMMARY

Amid many challenges, health systems and hospitals are striving to improve the health of their communities with varying degrees of commitment. While many have recognized the importance of the social determinants of health, most have not responded aggressively to the global climate crisis that is sickening and killing millions of people worldwide—and getting worse. As the largest healthcare provider in New York, Northwell Health is committed to keeping our communities well in the most socially responsible way. That means engaging with partners to enhance well-being, expand access to equitable care, and take environmental responsibility.

Healthcare organizations have a special obligation to broaden their efforts to prevent further damage to the planet and limit the human toll of that damage. For this to happen, their governing boards must support tangible environmental, social, and governance (ESG) strategies and put in place the administrative structures for their C-suites that are necessary to ensure compliance. At Northwell Health, governance is the engine that drives accountability for ESG.

HEALTHCARE ORGANIZATIONS OF all types have unique obligations and responsibilities. All articulate a commitment to improving health and well-being; they strive for excellence in treating illness, discovering new treatments and therapies, and educating their future workforce. They can be especially proud of their outstanding work in responding to COVID-19. Many can take credit for new initiatives to address aspects of the social determinants of health.

Now is the time to take broader and deeper actions to directly address the impact of climate change, especially because the healthcare sector is a major contributor to environmental damage. The data are clear: Emissions coming directly from US healthcare facilities and indirectly from the goods and services they rely on are higher than the emissions of any industrialized nation (Pichler et al. 2019) and are responsible for 27 percent of all greenhouse gases (GHGs) produced by healthcare facilities worldwide (Karliner et al. 2019).

ACTION STARTS WITH ACCOUNTABILITY

The vast majority of US hospitals and health systems are aware of their responsibility and their contributions to GHG emissions. They know their numbers, but very few disclose them. Most have modest internal goals that they are reluctant to share outside their organizations—and in too many cases, they do not even communicate them internally, as Northwell Health does.

Indeed, healthcare is already heavily regulated. Way too many mandates become unnecessarily burdensome; they frequently stifle innovation. But more mandates will be imposed unless all providers proactively report GHG emissions and outline plans for mitigating their practices. From a governance standpoint, healthcare leaders must make organizational commitments to hold themselves accountable by using corporate social responsibility (CSR) frameworks such as the Global Reporting Initiative (www.globalreporting.org/) and the Carbon Disclosure Project (www.cdp.net/en) standards for

GHG reporting. In making these commitments, healthcare leaders can be held to the same standards as leaders in industries that are required by regulatory oversight bodies to regularly report—and be held accountable.

Positive steps to accountability are being taken in healthcare. More than 60 providers, organizations, and associations representing the nation's largest health systems, including Northwell Health, signed the White House/Department of Health and Human Services Health Sector Climate Pledge in June 2022 to reduce GHG emissions by 50 percent by 2030. The pledge can be accessed at www.hhs.gov.

Achieving this goal requires more than lip service from CEOs and boards of directors. It must become their top organizational priority led by a seismic shift in philosophy and investments in management and structural capabilities, as well as a retreat from current practices that are responsible for aggravating health problems. An effectively purpose-driven mindset includes a vision for achieving stretch goals, creating internal policies to guide those efforts, establishing metrics for success, and, perhaps more importantly, educating and engaging the workforce every step of the way so that employees can be key contributors to the effort.

THE BENEFITS OF TAKING ACTION

In most communities, hospitals and healthcare providers are major drivers of the local economy and are the largest employers. Northwell Health is the largest private employer in New York. What providers say and how they act make a huge impact. They can be influencers for good. Their actions on climate change can have multiple benefits, such as

- inspiring, engaging, and energizing current staff, especially employees who desire to be part of a positive cause—more than 500 employees have joined Northwell Health's Green Business Employee Resource Group (GreenBERG) to advise on how the health system prioritizes sustainable and socially responsible initiatives;

- attracting new talent among the growing number of young professionals and middle-aged millennials who make employment decisions based on an organization's CSR interests and ESG rating;
- focusing on communities disproportionately affected by the effects of climate change, which supports efforts to promote health equity and address health disparities (Exhibit 1);
- making real the mission of improving overall health and making clear the belief that enhancing health is much more than providing good medical care—a guiding principle that is reinforced at Northwell Health in communication with employees, patients, and the community at large;
- influencing the behaviors of vendors, partners, and affiliates through financial might—in 2021 alone, Northwell Health procured $4.9 billion of supplies, pharmaceuticals, capital, and services from 15,000 vendors, including 1,700 small-, minority-, and veteran-owned businesses; and
- empowering the organization's commitment to employee wellness, equity, diversity, and inclusion.

GOOD GOVERNANCE MAKES IT REAL

Northwell Health's organizational structure ensures systemwide input, guidance, and accountability on CSR goals. This goes to

Exhibit 1: Northwell Health's Focus on 11 Most-Vulnerable Communities

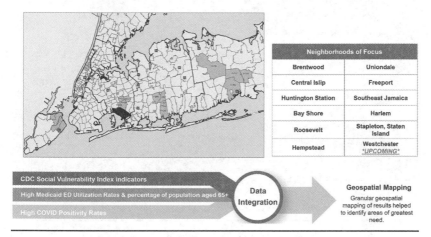

Neighborhoods of Focus	
Brentwood	Uniondale
Central Islip	Freeport
Huntington Station	Southeast Jamaica
Bay Shore	Harlem
Roosevelt	Stapleton, Staten Island
Hempstead	Westchester *UPCOMING*

CDC Social Vulnerability Index indicators

High Medicaid ED Utilization Rates & percentage of population aged 65+

High COVID Positivity Rates

Data Integration

Geospatial Mapping
Granular geospatial mapping of results helped to identify areas of greatest need.

Source: © Northwell Health. Used with permission.

Note: Northwell Health has targeted 11 priority communities to formalize relationships to expand healthcare access; increase screenings for chronic illness; and work with local leaders, businesses, and government agencies on social determinant issues such as housing, food insecurity, transportation, jobs, education, and safety.

the G in ESG. The structure mirrors the approach taken in disaster preparedness, pulling in resources and talent from all shared services across the organization as well as representatives from the local hospitals and other facilities who are on the front lines of day-to-day operations.

Northwell Health's website highlights four strategic CSR pillars: Environmental Responsibility & Sustainable Supply Chain; Excellence & Equity in Care; Community Partnerships; and Team Member Well-being, Equity, Diversity & Inclusion along with corporate priorities (www.northwell.edu/about-northwell/corporate -socialresponsibility). A multidisciplinary CSR governance team (Exhibit 2) sets strategies and goals based on input from stakeholders and then monitors real progress.

Exhibit 2: Core CSR Function with a Multidisciplinary CSR Governance Team

	Responsibilities:
Executive Sponsors	• Provide strategic vision and guidance • Be decision influencers and advocates
Core CSR Function	• Set strategy based on steering committee and other feedback • Provide governance, tracking and support • Manage program development, partnership criteria, and day to day execution

Steering Committee

• Community & Population Health • Center for Gun Violence Prevention • Center for Equity of Care • Marketing & Communications • Finance • Patient Experience	• Foundation • Sustainability • Center for Global Health • Legal & Compliance • Human Resources • Site/Operations	• Provide input on strategy and key decisions • Align on strategy communication and promotion

Source: © Northwell Health. Used with permission.

Note: CSR = corporate social responsibility.

Environmental Responsibility and Sustainable Supply Chain

Goals to decrease energy usage, emissions, and waste, and build a more sustainable supply chain include

- reducing GHG emissions by 50 percent by 2030;
- achieving net-zero emissions by 2050;
- lowering electricity use by 10 percent by 2027;
- increasing recycling volume to 25 percent of total waste volume by 2027;
- developing an inventory of supply chain emissions by the end of 2024;
- spending more with minority-, women-, and veteran-owned businesses to reach 10 percent of total spend with suppliers by 2026; and

- releasing a resilience plan for continuous operations by mid-2023, anticipating the needs of populations that experience a disproportionate risk of climate-related harm.

While pursuing these goals through a CSR framework, management created an environmental sustainability committee (Exhibit 3) in the spring of 2022 to advance a three-prong approach:

- **Mitigation.** Reduce the carbon imprint of Northwell Health's healthcare delivery system by leveraging supply chains to reduce all forms of waste. This includes buying locally sourced products where possible and purchasing reprocessed devices in specific clinical spaces.
- **Resiliency.** Operate healthcare facilities that can withstand the impact of climate change and other emergencies. This ensures the ability to continue operations and meet communities' healthcare needs.
- **Leadership.** Raise awareness and understanding of the health effects of climate change to both workers and communities through internal and public education efforts as well as advocacy for climate-smart policies at all levels of government.

Exhibit 3: Environmental Sustainability Committee Structure

Board	Internal Relationships and Environmental Groups
Executive Committee	GreenBERG
Steering Committee	Corporate Social Responsibility

		Practice Greenhealth
Ambulatory	Information Technology	
Biomedical Engineering	Marketing and Internal Communications	
Buildings and Infrastructure	Perioperative Services	Healthcare Without Harm
Clinical	Pharmacy	
Finance	Procurement	Healthcare Climate Council
Food and Nutrition	Research	
Hospital Operations	Shared Services	Institute for Healthcare Improvement
Human Resources	True North Enterprises	

Source: © Northwell Health. Used with permission.

The environmental sustainability committee comprises senior clinical and administrative leaders from various business areas at Northwell Health. The structure supports open dialogue on environmental sustainability across the organization. Members of the committee also have established relationships with organizations that share best practices and help guide corporate strategies, including Practice Greenhealth, Health Care Without Harm, the Health Care Climate Council, and the Institute for Healthcare Improvement.

The strategy for meeting environmental goals centers on 10 areas: Energy & Emissions, Greening the OR (operating room) & Procedural Areas, Green Purchasing, Waste Management, Food & Nutrition, Transportation, Greening Ambulatory, Sustainable IT (information technology), Clinical Sustainability, and Hospital Green Teams.

In each area, work groups led by senior-level executives are responsible for overseeing the respective sustainability efforts and monitoring progress throughout the Northwell Health system. That is a massive undertaking in an organization with a workforce of more than 81,000, 21 hospitals, more than 850 outpatient locations, a medical research institute, and one of the nation's largest academic teaching enterprises. The commitment involves nearly all departments within Northwell Health's shared services. The following points outline some environmental initiatives.

- Reduce GHG emissions, minimize energy waste, procure renewable energy, and implement clean energy practices at all existing facilities, and pursue LEED (leadership in energy and environmental design) certification on new building projects.
- Promote green laboratories, operating rooms, and other procedural areas by reprocessing and recycling materials.
- Pursue purchasing practices that support green cleaning, including hand hygiene and paper recycling; reduce the use of chemicals and water bottles; and eliminate the use of plastic.

- Reduce electronic, medical, pharmaceutical, clinical, and food waste; increase recycling at all facilities.
- Purchase locally produced food, standardize the use of eco-friendly food containers, and purchase sustainably farmed meats while also offering more nonmeat meal options.
- Purchase electric vehicles (EV), increase the number of EV charging stations, improve the efficiency of supply-chain distribution practices, and promote employee carpooling through rideshare credits and public transportation usage.
- Enhance IT sustainability with more energy-efficient equipment and electronics recycling.
- Rely more on environmentally friendly anesthetics, inhalers, and intubation kits.
- Use biodegradable personal protective equipment.

To ensure accountability with these initiatives, sustainability work groups report their progress at the bimonthly meetings of the environmental sustainability committee, which, in turn, communicates progress in each area to the GreenBERG and the CSR steering committee during bimonthly meetings. The board of trustees reviews periodic progress updates—detailed reports are presented biannually to the executive committee, every September to the quality committee, and annually to all trustees during their annual board retreat.

Excellence and Equity in Care and Community Partnerships

Northwell Health's work in promoting population health and responding to social determinant issues, as shown in Exhibit 4, is integrated into the corporate CSR strategy. A key starting point in ramping up efforts to address health disparities is collecting accurate racial–ethnic data and language preferences. In short, healthcare providers need to better understand the communities being served, including their vulnerabilities.

Northwell Health has developed several community partnerships and collaborations with local leaders (Exhibit 4) to identify needs and risk factors in underserved communities, including the 11 most-vulnerable neighborhoods as noted earlier.

To leverage these community partnerships, Northwell Health has set a goal of identifying and providing interventions that address the social needs of 500,000 people—specifically expanding access to care in underserved communities—by 2030. These priorities were established through a formal process involving interviews with internal leaders and external stakeholders, an employee survey, peer and leader benchmarking, and a series of workshops with the CSR committee to set the goals.

The same process to identify priorities was used to address upstream factors affecting community health, including a goal of increasing the social determinants of health screening rate to at least 50 percent by 2030. Other initiatives are:

Exhibit 4: Health Equity Collaborations

Community Initiatives Prioritized With the Community

Education	Economic Vitality	Neighborhood & Physical Environment	Health & Healthcare Disparities
• Northwell Community Scholars Program • FutureReady NYC • Cohen's Children's Medical Center School Programs • Medical School Pipeline Program • General Community Education • Center for Learning & Innovation Programs	• Supplier Diversity Initiatives • Workforce Readiness Programs • Employment Opportunities at Northwell • Financial Assistance Programs • Others	• Social Determinants of Health e.g., Food Insecurity, Transportation • Sustainability/Climate Change • Gun Violence Program • Human Trafficking Program • Tobacco Cessation Program • NY Islanders/Rangers Partnership • The Center for Global Health • Others	• Mental Health, Diabetes & Obesity, Maternal Health, Cancer • Access to Care: FQHCs, Belmont Clinic, Fire Island • Health Solutions Care Management and Health Home • General Outreach and Screening of chronic conditions • Public Health. COVID-19, Flu, Event Medicine

Initiatives and Programs

Source: © Northwell Health. Used with permission.

- educational programs for youth, which include mentoring and scholarship assistance;
- Food as Health and Wellness on Wheels programs that address food insecurity and poor nutrition;
- mental health services; and
- gun violence prevention and safety programs.

To ensure governance accountability, the board's committee on community health oversees the health system's community health strategy and meets quarterly to receive updates. Some Northwell Health hospitals also have their own community health committees that provide input on local needs. In addition, a community health needs assessment for our service area is compiled every three years and posted on the Northwell Health website.

Team Member Well-being

Following Northwell Health's corporate commitment to socially responsible care, CSR priorities must also ensure the well-being of employees. In addition to chaplaincy services, an employee assistance program, and Team Lavender peer-to-peer support, the Center for Traumatic Stress, Resilience and Recovery has provided emotional support and resources for employees and their families affected by COVID-19 and other stressors.

Another vital employee wellness effort promotes healthy lifestyles. In 2021, more than 50,000 employees were enrolled in Northwell Health's online wellness platform. The goal is to increase participation by 40 percent by 2025. Incentives include discounts on benefit costs for completing an annual health risk assessment and wellness competitions in which individuals and teams are rewarded for tracking their steps and participating in walking events.

CONCLUSION

Progress in responding to environmental challenges requires ongoing, dedicated, and concerted efforts with the administrative structures in place to ensure compliance. In short, it is a long journey. By acting now to prevent further damage to the environment, the healthcare sector can take a leading role to reduce the growth of associated health risks. Some of the damage is human-made, and humans can change it.

By applying sound governance practices, Northwell Health has made strides in that reduction, but there is much more to do. The ESG journey is a humbling experience where gaps and shortcomings become glaringly obvious on an ongoing basis. But healthcare has a large environmental and social footprint, and we as healthcare leaders have a corresponding responsibility through effective governance to do the right thing—to stay true to our mission of improving the health of the communities we serve. It is time to respond to this urgent call to action. We owe it to all future generations.

REFERENCES

Karliner, J., S. Slotterback, R. Boyd, B. Ashby, and K. Steele. 2019. "Health Care's Climate Footprint: How the Health Sector Contributes to the Global Climate Crisis, and Opportunities for Action." Health Care Without Harm Climate—Smart Health Care Series, Green Paper Number One. Produced in collaboration with Arup. Published September 2019. https://noharm -global.org/sites/default/files/documents-files/5961/Health CaresClimateFootprint_092319.pdf.

Pichler, P.-P., I. S Jaccard, U. Weisz, and H. Weisz. 2019. "International Comparison of Health Care Carbon Footprints." *Environmental Research Letters* 14 (6): 1–8. https://doi.org/10.1088 /1748-9326/ab19e1.

FOR DISCUSSION

1. Healthcare is already heavily regulated. So why should healthcare feel compelled to report its carbon footprint?
2. What is the rationale for engaging all employees— not just leaders—in organizational efforts to reduce greenhouse gas emissions?
3. Who are the stakeholders that healthcare leaders should call upon to identify and provide social needs interventions for their communities?

ESG Expands the View of Corporate Stewardship in Healthcare

MICHELE BAKER RICHARDSON, JD

SUMMARY

At Advocate Aurora Health, the board of directors established parameters for effectively executing the governance (G) function related to ESG activities while adopting a comprehensive approach to ESG that includes the corporate commitment to health equity. Establishing a board diversity, equity, and inclusion (DEI) committee with external experts served to integrate these efforts with the ESG strategy. This approach will continue to guide the board of directors of Advocate Health, formed in December 2022, by the combination of Advocate Aurora Health and Atrium Health. Our experience has demonstrated that empowering individual board committee members of not-for-profit healthcare organizations to embrace their unique responsibility for driving ESG requires collective efforts in the boardroom as well as a commitment to board refreshment and diversity.

WHAT DOES IT mean to be a good steward?

The leader of our new members class at the church that my husband and I recently joined posed that question. Our answer was a "textbook definition" centered on the careful management of resources—a concept of stewardship that also is the foundation of the responsibilities of board directors throughout the United States.

Directors work to ensure the sustainability of organizations through strategic oversight by establishing metrics to hold leaders accountable. Primarily, directors have interpreted this responsibility as a requirement to monitor the financial performance of management (Otto, De Renzy Channer, and Summerfield 2022). More recently, the conversation around stewardship in boardrooms across the country has become a much richer one that evaluates the spectrum of possible risks that could affect sustainability in a company's operations.

Investors' evolving sophistication and social consciousness have underscored several additional risks that make an impact on balance sheets in the for-profit world. Investors today are attracted to organizations that reliably take care of the environment and their people—workforce and consumers—because these organizations are more likely to be profitable (Kell 2018). In short, organizations that do good are also doing well financially. As such, directors in the for-profit world are applying an environmental, social, and governance (ESG) framework to assess their organization's ability to achieve its objectives and respond to the market demand for increased attention to ESG.

Even with the mission-driven nature of most not-for-profit organizations, however, the healthcare sector has lagged behind its for-profit counterparts when discussing, articulating, and implementing a clear and comprehensive ESG strategy (PNC 2022). While there is little dispute about the merits of certain goals that fall under the ESG umbrella (e.g., carbon neutrality), significant economic headwinds in the world of not-for-profit healthcare have left management and directors questioning the pace at which their organizations can address critical investments both in the core infrastructure *and* in the ESG-related items.

Much of the initial attention in healthcare has been placed on the environmental and social aspects of ESG, and yet the board's role in governance is equally important because of the connection of its role to safety, health outcomes, and the workforce pipeline. The short lesson from the deep examination of both the E and the S for the not-for-profit sector is that interest in E and S is good for business and good for patients and communities.

THE PURVIEW OF DIRECTORS

The main concerns related to the governance issues in ESG involve the decisions and responsibilities that fall squarely within the purview of directors. Governance in healthcare is typically responsible for areas such as

- approving the organization's strategic mission and plans to achieve it;
- partnering with the CEO and senior management to establish meaningful metrics to achieve results, appropriately incentivize management, and monitor progress toward goals;
- assessing key risks to the organization and considering their potential impact on patients, team members, and communities; and
- electing qualified directors and determining the appropriate committee structure to accomplish the work together (in other words, establishing who sits around the board table).

Working effectively to address each of these responsibilities has the potential to advance ESG goals.

For example, before Advocate Aurora Health's combination with Atrium Health, Advocate Aurora Health's board was already engaged in each of these areas without explicitly labeling them under the ESG umbrella. The board directed its energy toward the goal of addressing health disparities in the system's footprint and established a separate diversity, equity, and inclusion (DEI) committee in 2019 with its own charter and several independent committee members. The work of this committee continues to include interfacing with a senior staff-led DEI work group. (Shortly after establishing the DEI committee, the board voted to also include DEI oversight language in the charters of each board committee through the governance committee.) We did this all at Advocate Aurora Health without explicitly labeling that work ESG. However, after our strategic planning retreat where we heard from industry experts on ESG, we began to view our health equity work more in the context of ESG.

The topic of ESG emerged on the retreat agenda at the request of board members who served on other boards of for-profit entities and were interested in its application in the not-for-profit healthcare sector. Most of the board members could articulate the definitions of E, S, and G. However, clear articulation of how ESG related to our roles as health system board members responsible for the long-term sustainability of our enterprise was more of a challenge. Until that retreat, ESG was treated mainly as a compliance issue focused on environmental stewardship and, to a lesser extent, on recent societal factors such as the COVID-19 pandemic. Post retreat, we took a comprehensive view of the ESG-identified risks, amended those committee charters once again, and assigned committee oversight to each of those risks.

Moreover, we began to have a different conversation about DEI in the context of ESG. We began to talk about the critical importance of DEI in achieving our organization's safety goals, which are critical to patient satisfaction, and other metrics that bear on the bottom line. Understanding DEI objectives as a business imperative represented a shift in our collective thinking. When viewed through this lens, a discussion about the system's seemingly straightforward mission statement ("We Help People Live Well") became not so simple.

An inclusive, deliberative process in the early days of the new organization led to an honest discussion between governance and management about what might be required to achieve that goal for *all* those we helped. That evolved into a deep organizational commitment to achieving health equity not only for current patients but also for everyone within our service area. As an organization with deep faith and community roots, all of us were comfortable with the notion of reasonable service, but we continued to be challenged by what might be considered "reasonable service" in the face of difficult financial headwinds. In a game of scarcity where margins are eroding and reimbursement is decreasing, we continued to revisit the conundrum of how to do good *and* to do well.

ELEMENTS OF GOOD GOVERNANCE

To begin, our discussion would not have been possible without several structural elements in place to ensure effective governance.

Starting from the Top

No discussion can effectively take place to advance all elements of ESG in healthcare without a transparent and courageous CEO. Leadership at the top requires a recognition that the ground is shifting. These shifts were never more apparent than with the onset of the COVID-19 pandemic. As corporate governance is entrusted with the evaluation of the CEO, it is valuable to consider not only results-driven metrics but also qualitative metrics that assess how a CEO accomplishes their work. Engaging in comprehensive evaluations in which how a CEO leads is as important as what the CEO's team achieves recognizes the reality that a CEO who models values such as compassion, curiosity, transparency, innovation, and commitment can make a positive impact on organizational culture, talent recruitment and retention, and ultimately on the bottom line.

Establishing Leadership Principles

During our first governance meeting at Advocate Aurora Health, the new board chair and I proposed some rules of engagement that we all agreed to in principle. These included rules such as "seek first to understand and then to be understood" and "assume goodwill." We would return to these guiding principles repeatedly as we listened to new perspectives and articulated our own. Generally, directors are very comfortable evaluating objective data and information but are considerably less comfortable challenging the assumptions behind the data. Time spent together in a nonmeeting setting (e.g., a strategic retreat) according to our rules of engagement helped facilitate those conversations.

Making Courage Contagious

Encouraging all to share a view by inviting participation from each board member is also helpful. Encouraging and asking for dissenting views is an effective tactic, always seeking first to understand and assuming goodwill. For example, when considering capital allocation decisions, the evaluation of return on investment on a project is typically a formulaic discussion that may or may not consider community needs and impact assessments. Ensuring that financial, political, community, and diversity risks are included in the assessment methodology and conversation can lead to a more robust conversation about how we examine value.

Living the Complexities: Trust but Verify

Reliance on the expertise of those in management is the best way to lead the discussion about strategy. The CEO and senior leadership team live the complexities that exist within an organization each day and have deep, valuable perspectives that boards can learn from. The best leaders also have a broad strategic vision, and they welcome challenges and questions that clarify and build upon—or perhaps even help dismantle—existing models and assumptions based on experience from other industries. In addition, both management and governance leaders can benefit from the perspective of external advisers who can zoom out and help all open their aperture to take a much wider view of possible solutions to seemingly intractable problems.

DATA COLLECTION AND THE CONNECTION TO HEALTH EQUITY

In terms of establishing appropriate metrics and measuring progress toward ESG goals, the board's commitment to asking the right questions about the type of data collected can help drive progress. For example, at Advocate Aurora Health, surveying patients and collecting appropriate data enabled better treatment of patients and prevented future harm. To ensure that the organization could access these vital insights, the board approved strategic infrastructure investments in the proper systems to provide real-time feedback to caregivers. This foundational change was a type of ESG investment. Importantly, we learned that it was not simply about investing in the feedback system but also about ensuring that we had the right talent in place to ask patients the right questions in the correct language—and in a culturally appropriate manner to ensure the best outcomes.

Directors across the nation have joined together with thought partners to share best practices in governance to reduce inequities in healthcare, and that effort has been generously supported by many of the health systems leading the way in health equity and ESG. At its most recent national meeting attended by directors from some of the most forward-thinking organizations across the

US health system, the Black Directors Health Equity Agenda presented its seminal work, produced in partnership with Deloitte, including a playbook for directors and an ESG preview to equip directors with the relevant questions and structures to advance health equity by connecting with larger ESG efforts (https://bdhea .org/offerings/).

MANAGEMENT INCENTIVES

Directors are charged with providing appropriate incentives to management through the long- and short-term programs that drive important outcomes. The adage "What gets measured, gets done" has never been truer. Reaching targeted financials is always an appropriate metric to consider when ensuring sustainability.

In the Advocate Aurora Health system, the system-wide safety metric (a composite score of the most relevant measures over time to drive safer health outcomes) has proved to be essential. Given the success of using these metrics, the board decided under the guidance of the DEI committee to add a DEI metric, which is also a composite score. This score is based on those factors that will improve health outcomes and reduce disparities in care. It includes patient experience scores that are detailed by the race and gender of our patients. Scoring has helped identify and correct discrepancies in supplier diversity and the diversity of slates for hiring.

BOARD REFRESHMENT AND DIVERSITY

The vital role of governance is also emphasized in the robust process of board refreshment and evaluation. Board evaluations have been the norm at Advocate Aurora Health, and we took the industry standard step of establishing term limits for directors. Initially, evaluations were done with the assistance of an outside party and were anonymous—we were still getting to know each other and it was important that the directors felt that they could be honest and open in sharing feedback. In subsequent years, board evaluations have been conducted internally, and they have allowed us to adjust our meeting schedule to allow more time for strategic discussion. In the most recent iteration, we began the process of self-evaluation and completed a skills matrix to determine whether any skills were missing in the boardroom.

Advisers also helped us at Advocate Aurora Health to consider the important criteria for the CEO of a future, aspirational organization. We carefully revisited those criteria as we considered potential partners. Other board directors who are serious about board refreshment will need to be open to a similar process that will help identify the skill sets needed to effectively govern.

With the use of term limits and transparent feedback, board directors can become a governance body that is prepared to address the issues facing the health system of the future. Everyone sitting in a board seat should be thinking about a person with the skill sets and diverse experiences who could succeed him or her. Board membership needs to be inclusive and flexible to ensure that those best equipped to ask the right questions will be seated at the table.

Facing the Future

Among the many issues facing the healthcare board of the future is the diversity of the patient population that it will be called to serve. Given the current makeup of boards at most major hospital systems (The Leverage Network 2021), it will be mission-critical to address gaps in the demographics and include members who are able to ask the right questions about high-impact issues such as disparities in care delivery. These topics are important because they can affect other issues such as safety ratings and the ability to recruit the best talent with an appropriately wide range of experiences.

CONCLUSION

Ultimately, board members with a variety of experiences and perspectives who reflect patient populations will be in the best position to provide wise counsel and partnership to an organization's leaders during turbulent times.

For the foreseeable future, the challenges in healthcare will require creative and community-centered solutions that rely on the best possible governance to work alongside management. Together, they can form the necessary framework for success and hold each other accountable. Getting the G right in ESG is where the work begins and sets the stage for addressing both the E and the S effectively in the healthcare setting and beyond.

REFERENCES

Kell, G. 2018. "The Remarkable Rise of ESG." *Forbes.* Published June 11. https://www.forbes.com/sites/georgkell/2018/07/11/theremarkable-rise-of-esg/?sh=406c54161695.

Otto, F., R. De Renzy Channer, and A. Summerfield. 2022. "Boards Stepping Up as Stewards of Sustainability." *Harvard Law School Forum on Corporate Governance.* Published November 20. https://corpgov.law.harvard.edu/2022/11/20/boards-stepping-up-as-stewards-of-sustain ability/.

PNC. 2022. "Social Responsibility Initiatives Taking Hold in For-Profit and Nonprofit Organizations, PNC Survey Shows." Published March 22. https://pnc.mediaroom.com/PNCIAM-socialresponsibility-survey.

The Leverage Network. 2021. "Iniquity Starts at the Top." Published February 21. https://theleveragnetworkinc.com/inequity-starts-at-the-top-wp-2/.

FOR DISCUSSION

1. How have board responsibilities evolved over the years beyond fiduciary concerns?
2. How can diversity, equity, and inclusion interests fit into your organization's ESG framework?
3. In an ESG context, what valuable qualities should a board look for in its CEO?
4. What are the potential benefits of having a board that reflects the local population?

The Disparity Challenge: How Governance Can Lead the Way on Diversity, Equity, and Inclusion

ANTOINETTE HARDY-WALLER, MJ, RN

SUMMARY

Hospitals, health systems, pharmaceutical companies, device makers, and payers have a responsibility to provide high-quality, innovative, cost-effective care and services to their patients and communities. The governing boards of these institutions provide the vision, strategy, and resources and choose the best leaders to achieve those outcomes. Healthcare boards can play a vital role in ensuring that resources are distributed where they are most needed. The need is great in communities of racial and ethnic diversity, which are almost always underserved—a preexisting condition that came into stark relief during the COVID-19 pandemic. Widespread inequities in access to care, housing, nutrition, and other components of good health were documented, and boards promised to pursue change, including becoming more diverse themselves. More than two years later, healthcare boards and senior executives remain mostly white and male. This continuing reality is especially unfortunate

> because diversity in governance and the C-suite has positive implications for financial, operational, and clinical success, including solving persistent inequities and disparities experienced in disadvantaged communities.

HEALTHCARE GOVERNING BOARDS often work out of public view, yet they play a significant role in ensuring that the quality, safety, and cost-effectiveness of patient care are the highest that the organization can achieve. An effective board guides management; establishes mission, vision, and values; confirms and implements corporate strategy; and monitors organizational performance and finance. Boards that govern successfully also assess their own performance, continuously making improvements in how they function.

Following the height of the pandemic and the murder of George Floyd in May 2020, a social justice movement took hold throughout much of the United States. Healthcare was frequently cited as "Exhibit A" in shortfalls in diversity, equity, and inclusion (DEI). Blacks and other people of color had far more COVID-19 cases, hospitalizations, and deaths than whites; less access to insurance, transportation, and all the other elements of good health; and no way to socially isolate. Healthcare boards, which are responsible for meeting the healthcare needs of their communities, have historically had low representation of racial, ethnic, and gender diversity, although the latter has improved marginally.

To identify the correlation between board diversity and the persistence of health disparities, The Leverage Network, the Health Equity Leadership Pipeline Collaborative at the University of Michigan School of Public Health, and the legal and consulting firm McGuire-Woods conducted a retrospective study of 623 board members at 41 of the largest healthcare organizations in the United States across the provider, payer, pharmaceutical, and biotech markets from 2016 to 2018. This research found that the average board was 87 percent white and 13 percent of people of color. Seventy-two percent of members were male, and only 3 percent were Black women. Among CEOs, the picture was even bleaker: Blacks held just 8.5 percent of the top jobs, and women held only 4 percent. There was not a single Black female healthcare CEO in the study group (The Leverage Network 2021).

VALUABLE ADVANTAGES

Organizations with culturally competent boards and leaders gain an advantage over less diverse organizations by offering superior services to their communities. In a survey of 311 healthcare executives across the United States conducted by the search firm Witt/Kieffer, 71 percent of respondents agreed that having culturally diverse perspectives on healthcare boards leads to successful decision-making (Gauss and Tomlin 2015).

Healthcare trustees who understand the root causes, issues, needs, and cultures of their patients can provide business insights that result in better decision-making regarding expanded access to care and support services such as transportation assistance. They also may have connections with other community leaders who can help hospitals and health systems address local social determinants of health and help achieve community health goals. In addition, diverse and inclusive healthcare boards report richer discussions with broader perspectives that help their organizations avoid missteps in implementing new programs and services for patient populations. Such missteps could include under-resourcing current offerings and adding new ones to meet the needs of the communities served.

A board that maintains diverse perspectives is better informed because its members can leverage their unique life experiences to affect board decisions. These perspectives lead to robust discussions and allow the board to develop a more nuanced understanding of how to provide patient-centered services in accordance with the unique needs of communities.

It is also worth noting that there is also a more traditional financial return on investment in equity. Companies in the top quartile for ethnic and cultural diversity are 36 percent more likely to outperform those in the bottom quartile, with an average operating margin of 12 percent compared with 8 percent among entities with homogeneous boards (McKinsey & Company 2020).

Exhibit 1 suggests a basic process for establishing inclusive governance.

HIDDEN IN PLAIN SIGHT

There are many stories of healthcare boards and senior leaders being pressed by staff, faculty, and local communities to add different voices but failing to find a single minority candidate who meets their

Exhibit 1: A DEI Starter List

Strategy
Understand the organization's current diversity and inclusion environment.

Talent
Educate yourself on inclusion and inclusive governance.

Governance
Begin embedding inclusion into all board processes.

Integrity
With management, concretely define what inclusion means and behaviors that support it.

Performance
Prioritize inclusion as a strategic imperative on the board's agenda; monitor relevant metrics.

Source: Adapted from Fucci and Cooper (2019).

criteria. In response to this failure, The Leverage Network annually convenes more than 500 Black executives with the leadership skills and experience to serve on a board. Of course, they learn what good governance is all about, but mainly they learn how to overcome the biggest obstacle to minority advancement: the "hiding in plain sight" phenomenon.

People who talk about a dearth of Black leaders who are ready for board roles may be surprised to learn that there are thousands of Black leaders with top credentials ready to lead. Whether it is from unconscious bias or cultural differences, they are simply unseen by white leaders. They may not fit with someone's vision of what a CEO or board chair should look or sound like, but until these diverse leaders are seen, heard, and given opportunities, the severe lack of diverse representation in key decision-making roles will continue at a time when it is so important to have it.

Rather than just waiting to be found, many Black executives promote themselves for healthcare board opportunities. They turn to programs such as The Leverage Network's Healthcare Board Initiative for coaching and networking. In addition, these executives learn how to bring an equity lens into the boardroom and leverage their unique experiences to directly influence decisions around equity.

A HIGHER LEVEL

Bringing diversity to the board is an achievement, but then it is time to make a difference. Leaders of color bring their life experiences to the table, having faced the same obstacles and subconscious bias that people in disadvantaged communities face every day. Board members who are sensitive to issues affecting service to diverse patients can move governance to a higher level. They push back during board conversations, offering perspectives that broaden the board's thinking.

"As a board chair, I know this much for sure: Board members are kidding themselves—indeed [being] derelict—if they consider it sufficient to squeeze in a once-annual update from a chief diversity officer, and that accounts for their DEI efforts," says Chris Lowney, chair of the board of CommonSpirit Health. "True diversity means transforming the whole organization—from who is in the boardroom, to whom we hire, to caregiver practices, to community outreach. Transformation of large organizations only happens when the CEO and board members are personally committed to driving the transformation themselves, including the issue of who sits around the board and senior management table" (personal communication).

INCLUSION IN THE EQUATION

Diversity is just one part of the DEI equation. Boards must have an interest in encouraging inclusion as well. The uplift organizations receive from having an inclusive culture—not just a diverse workforce—is substantial. Where an inclusive culture exists, employees are likely to see themselves as part of a high-performing, collaborative, team-oriented organization.

As a first step in establishing accountability for inclusive governance practices, boards may consider establishing a committee, either temporary or permanent, that is dedicated to inclusion. This committee's mandate can be to elevate inclusion's visibility in the boardroom and promote inclusive governance practices across all board committees and procedures.

COMMONSPIRIT HEALTH: A DEI SUCCESS STORY

CommonSpirit Health operates 140 hospitals and more than 1,000 care sites in 21 states, representing some of the most diverse communities across the United States. The organization was formed in 2019 from the merger of two legacy Catholic health systems, Catholic Health Initiatives and Dignity Health, each led by a Black CEO in Kevin E. Lofton, FACHE, and Lloyd Dean, respectively. Their natural commitments to the elimination of health disparities are easily aligned with the mission of Catholic healthcare to serve the most vulnerable.

This heritage of caring put the new CommonSpirit Health board in a unique position to establish a mission that embodied a degree of equity and social justice that could make a real difference in the lives of those being served. The board's engagement and leadership in this work set the standard for how DEI would be viewed throughout the organization.

The board approved the 2026 Strategic Roadmap after a nine-month process of discernment. The road map includes three strategic pillars—"Our People, Our Excellence, and Our Future"—to support the new entity's mission, vision, and values. A commitment to DEI is built into each pillar. Today, the CommonSpirit Health board composition is 58 percent female and 42 percent people of racial–ethnic diversity. This intentional diversity is the key to activating the road map and realizing the system's full potential.

The health equity work at CommonSpirit Health is a collaborative effort that crosses every area of the organization. It is strategic and intentional and monitored by the board. In fact, health equity is embedded in each board agenda; metrics on the board's dashboard and results are factored into management's incentive plan.

Commitment to diversity also played out in the search in early 2022 for a new CommonSpirit CEO after Dean announced his retirement. Wayne Lassiter III, formerly CEO of Henry Ford Health, was chosen as the third consecutive Black CEO to serve the system.

As a result of all of these efforts, CommonSpirit Health was recognized by *Modern Healthcare* magazine as a "2022 Top Diversity Organization."

Diversity alone will not enable a board to optimize its effectiveness. Diversity paired with inclusion can make all members feel valued. The opinions of new board members should be actively sought, whether through discussions or on committees. And when new members are encouraged to share their perspectives, their input should be used in decision-making.

Many boards provide formal mentoring for new members. Through one-on-one meetings, mentors gain knowledge of the expertise and life experience that new members can offer. Standard tasks for the mentor could include making sure that the new member has received an information packet prior to a board meeting, checking whether the member has questions before or after a meeting, and confirming whether the member can log onto any online board portal. In addition, all established trustees should introduce themselves to establish a personal connection.

CONCLUSION

In any discussion of environmental, social, and governance (ESG) factors in healthcare delivery, the G in ESG should not be overlooked. A full appreciation of governance risks and opportunities in decision-making and practice is critical, as poor corporate governance practices have led to the downfall of enlightened organizations.

In the prioritization of governance decisions, three additional letters—DEI—have rightly achieved a high profile, with many stakeholders demanding better representation of women and people of color on boards and in executive ranks. More and more healthcare providers are seeing the value of responding to those demands and creating more inclusive systems. Integrating ESG into how an organization does business and delivers on its mission starts at the top with a robust governance structure that is committed to those ESG efforts.

REFERENCES

Fucci, M., and T. Cooper. 2019. "The Inclusion Imperative for Boards: Redefining Board Responsibilities to Support Organizational Inclusion." *Deloitte Insights*. Published April 2, 2019. www2.deloitte.com/us/en/insights/topics/value-of-diversity -and-inclusion/redefining-board-responsibilities-to-support -organizationalinclusion.html.

Gauss, J. W., and O. B. Tomlin III. 2015. "Closing the Gap in Healthcare Leadership Diversity: A Witt/Kieffer Study." www .wittkieffer.com/webfoo/wp-content/uploads/Closing-the-Gap -inHealthcare-Leadership-Diversity-Final.pdf.

McKinsey & Company. 2020. "Diversity Wins: How Inclusion Matters." Published May 19, 2020. www.mckinsey.com /featured-insights/diversity-and-inclusion/diversity-wins-how -inclusionmatters.

The Leverage Network. 2021. "Inequity Starts at the Top." https:// theleveragenetworkinc.com/wpcontent/uploads/2021/02 /Inequity-Starts-AtThe-Top-WP.pdf.

FOR DISCUSSION

1. Why has healthcare frequently been cited as "Exhibit A" in diversity, equity, and inclusion shortfalls?
2. What value does cultural diversity bring to healthcare boards?
3. Diversity alone is not enough. How can board leadership ensure that all board members feel a genuine sense of inclusion in governance? How do these actions advance ESG goals?

Integrating ESG, Sustainability, and Social Responsibility into Operations

MONICA L. NAKIELSKI

SUMMARY

Healthcare leaders have two especially profound responsibilities. In addition to ensuring quality, they must also drive sustainable practices that benefit their organizations, communities, and the planet. Environmental, social, and governance (ESG) principles—along with sustainability and corporate social responsibility (CSR) concepts—are gaining prominence, and an understanding of their nuances within healthcare and in the general business context is essential for effective governance and implementation. To fully integrate ESG principles into their operations, healthcare leaders need to understand the essential role of governance in ESG and the key differences among ESG, sustainability, and CSR. The concrete examples provided here will illustrate the relevance of ESG reporting frameworks to healthcare operations.

THE TERMS *ESG, sustainability,* and *CSR* are often used interchangeably. While they represent interconnected ideas, they are distinct.

- **ESG** refers to a broad set of environmental, social, and governance considerations that leaders should apply in their organizational decision-making processes. ESG encompasses carbon emissions, resource management, labor practices, diversity, stakeholder relationships, internal controls, and ethical conduct. These areas have gained significant importance in recent years as more investors recognize the value of incorporating environmental and social considerations into their investment decisions, driving businesses to integrate them within their operations.
- **Sustainability** more broadly encompasses the needs of the present without compromising the ability of future generations to meet their own needs. It involves taking actions that cover economic, environmental, and social considerations equally.
- **CSR** focuses on an organization's commitment to making a positive impact on society through employee volunteerism and philanthropy. Integrating ethical behavior that extends beyond compliance with applicable rules and regulations exemplifies CSR.

While ESG is a standardized framework for sustainable decision-making, sustainability and CSR provide context and aspiration for organizations that want to operate responsibly.

ESG: GOOD FOR HEALTH, GOOD FOR BUSINESS

Because the E, S, and G in ESG are interconnected, they collectively make an impact on the long-term sustainability of hospitals and healthcare systems. Addressing ESG strategically and with a long-term mindset can lead to improved operational efficiency. Comparing data from 2001 and 2014, researchers have found that average revenue and earnings growth rates were 47 percent and 36 percent higher in 2014, respectively, and market capitalization grew faster, too (Barton, Manyika, and Williamson 2017).

The broad spectrum of ESG in healthcare inevitably leads to opportunities for healthcare leaders to address multiple impact dimensions simultaneously. Some examples follow.

- **Energy costs and patient well-being.** Investing in and implementing energy-efficient HVAC systems reduces environmental impact and leads to cost savings that can be reinvested in patient care, thus enhancing the social dimension of healthcare operations. Improved HVAC systems help improve patient outcomes and staff well-being with cleaner air.
- **Diversity and innovation.** Promoting diversity and inclusion through good governance heightens the social dimension by fostering a culture of equity and equal opportunity for staff. Also, a diverse workforce supports innovation by bringing a variety of perspectives to problem-solving.
- **Digital health and data privacy.** Digital health solutions such as telemedicine can improve access to care and enhance the social dimension. Simultaneously, robust data privacy safeguards, regulatory compliance, and transparent data practices reinforce the governance aspect of healthcare operations.
- **Data management and social responsibility.** A strong data governance program that oversees how a health system uses data not only protects valuable assets in compliance with applicable law but also ensures that the organization is entering into relationships with third parties that share its responsibility to patients and the wider community.

GOVERNANCE IN THE HEALTHCARE SECTOR

As the G in ESG, governance plays a vital role in effective decision-making, risk management, and ethical behavior through structure, policies, and processes.

Good governance in healthcare is fundamental for ensuring accountability and transparency. By establishing clear lines of responsibility and decision-making processes, healthcare leaders can uphold ethical standards and codes of conduct, thus strengthening public trust. An example of this is when hospitals and clinics establish governance structures that include oversight committees responsible for mitigating risks, monitoring ethical guidelines, and prioritizing patient care.

As Chrissa Pagitsas, author of the book *Chief Sustainability Officers at Work,* notes, "Integrating ESG into the risk management and governance framework is an advancement for businesses in all industries. It represents an enhanced 'risk identification toolbox' which now includes environmental risk, social risk, and governance risk" (personal communication, May 2023).

Assessing Risks and Opportunities

Healthcare leaders can draw from various toolboxes, described here, to help them systematically identify and address ESG risks and opportunities in their organizations.

- **ESG risk assessment.** This assessment evaluates operations, supply chain, and stakeholder relationships to identify potential ESG risks and their impact. An ESG risk assessment typically considers a wide range of factors such as climate change, human rights, labor practices, corporate governance, and community relations.

- **Materiality assessment.** A materiality assessment spots ESG issues that are most relevant to a company's operations, strategy, and stakeholders. By considering the significance of different ESG factors, leaders can prioritize their risk identification efforts and allocate resources effectively.
- **Scenario analysis.** In a scenario analysis, different future situations are developed and assessed to understand how ESG risks and opportunities may affect an organization. By considering various potential outcomes and their implications, organizations can identify and prepare for ESG-related risks that may arise in different scenarios.
- **Stakeholder input.** Engagement with employees, customers, investors, and communities can help identify ESG risks and opportunities. Stakeholders can provide valuable insights into the potential social and environmental effects of operations and help uncover risks that may not be immediately apparent.
- **ESG data and analytics.** ESG data and analytics tools provide quantitative and qualitative information on various ESG factors. These tools enable organizations to track and analyze ESG performance, identify emerging trends, and spot potential risks or areas for improvement.
- **ESG ratings and indices.** ESG ratings and indices evaluate companies based on their performance against ESG criteria. These tools can help organizations benchmark their ESG performance against industry peers, identify areas of weakness, and prioritize risk management efforts.
- **Regulatory and legal compliance review.** Organizations can use tools that provide updates and guidance on ESG-related laws, regulations, and reporting requirements. These tools can help identify and resolve compliance risks associated with ESG issues, such as environmental regulations or data privacy laws.

According to Pagitsas, the issues being raised through ESG historically have not been fully evaluated. Businesses in the technology manufacturing sector are now evaluating more deeply the social issue of human rights and whether their supply chain is using forced labor to manufacture their products, while agriculture and food production businesses face environmental issues related to the usage of water for crops (personal communication, May 2023). These examples highlight risks that in the past may have been in the background of business company strategies; today, they have equal standing with risks such as information technology stability, regulatory risk, and changing consumer trends. Addressing these risks now through strong governance can help to protect companies in the long run. A good executive team is looking to anticipate and mitigate risks five to ten years ahead, exploring ways to reduce costs, finding renewable energy sources, and refining the supply chain to enhance resiliency and limit the risks that can drive up costs. The sum, Pagitsas maintains, is a better operating company that is more likely to achieve a higher valuation and greater profitability.

FRAMING ESG INTEGRATION INTO HEALTHCARE OPERATIONS

Bon Secours Mercy Health provides a successful example of ESG integration on its website (https://bsmhealth.org/esg/). One of the national Catholic health ministry's key ESG performance indicators is "empower and enhance market board fiduciary engagement in clinical and quality fiduciary oversight through revision of market bylaws after consultation with market board leadership from across the system." One measure that ties board and leadership oversight to successful operations is the establishment of an ESG and Sustainability Council (Exhibit 1).

Healthcare compliance programs are required by the federal government and frame essential elements that include ongoing operational assessments to mitigate reputational, financial, and legal risks.

Exhibit 1: Bon Secours Mercy Health ESG and Sustainability Council Structure and Internal Stakeholder Participation

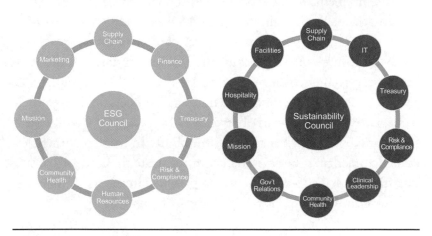

Source: Advantus Health Partners. Used with permission.

The strategic application of this assessment framework is gaining recognition as an efficient and collaborative way to incorporate ESG into a system's risk program. According to Cecilia DeLoach Lynn, director of sustainability performance and recognition at Practice Greenhealth, a nonprofit organization that promotes environmental stewardship, more sustainability leaders at healthcare organizations are asking about how to talk to compliance and finance colleagues and coach them on how to reframe their work for greater efficiencies and impact (personal communication, May 2023).

Several governance frameworks and standards exist to guide healthcare organizations in integrating ESG principles. The Global Reporting Initiative (www.globalreporting.org), Sustainability Accounting Standards Board (https://sasb.org), and Task Force on Climate-related Financial Disclosures (www.fsb-tcfd.org) are widely recognized for guidance on ESG reporting. Their frameworks help organizations measure, disclose, and manage ESG-related risks and opportunities.

To set a global baseline of sustainability disclosures to meet the needs of investors and financial markets, the International

Sustainability Standards Board harmonized the various frameworks and in June 2023 published its first two finalized standards: S1 General Requirements for Disclosure of Sustainability-related Financial Information and S2 Climate-related Disclosures (www.ifrs.org/issued-standards/ifrs-sustainability-standards-navigator).

By adopting cohesive, established ESG standards, healthcare leaders can readily enhance the transparency of their sustainability efforts, benchmark their performance against peers, and align their strategies with global goals. They can assess progress, identify areas for improvement, and ensure accountability in implementing sustainable practices. They can then communicate their organizations' initiatives to stakeholders, including patients, investors, employees, and the community.

CREATING VALUE WITH ESG

In today's healthcare landscape, patients can choose healthcare providers that prioritize sustainability and environmental stewardship. Investors, too, have an interest in supporting companies that align with their values and are seeking out organizations that exhibit responsible and sustainable practices. By meeting these expectations, healthcare organizations can enhance their brand reputation, attract capital, and differentiate themselves in the market. Business value is at stake when leaders can integrate social and environmental trends into their business strategy and decision-making.

The following points highlight the business imperative and value of leading ESG initiatives in healthcare operations:

- **Enhanced reputation.** Embracing strong governance practices and incorporating ESG principles can enhance a healthcare organization's reputation. It demonstrates a commitment to responsible business practices and can help build trust with patients, employees, investors, and other stakeholders.

- **Improved risk management.** Robust governance practices help healthcare organizations identify and manage risks effectively. By integrating ESG considerations into their decision-making processes, healthcare companies can mitigate potential financial, legal, operational, and reputational risks. This includes assessing risks related to climate change, public health crises, data privacy, and patient safety.
- **Attracting and retaining talent.** The healthcare industry faces intense competition for skilled professionals. A sharp ESG focus, including good governance, can help attract and retain top talent who are seeking employers with a commitment to sustainability, ethics, and social responsibility.
- **Access to capital.** Investors, rating agencies, and other financial stakeholders are increasingly incorporating ESG factors into their investment decisions. Healthcare organizations that demonstrate a commitment to ESG practices may have better access to capital as investors recognize the long-term value and stability associated with sustainable and well-governed businesses.
- **Operational efficiency.** Implementing ESG practices, including governance enhancements, can drive operational efficiencies within healthcare organizations. For example, by focusing on energy efficiency, waste management, and responsible supply chain practices, healthcare companies can reduce costs, optimize resource utilization, and minimize environmental impacts.

- **Patient and community engagement.** Healthcare organizations have a unique opportunity to positively affect patient outcomes and the communities they serve. By prioritizing governance and ESG principles, healthcare providers can build strong relationships with their patients and communities, leading to improved health outcomes, patient satisfaction, and community support.
- **Regulatory compliance.** Good governance practices help healthcare organizations comply with a wide range of regulations and standards. By adopting strong governance frameworks, healthcare companies can ensure compliance with healthcare laws, data privacy regulations, and other requirements, reducing legal and regulatory risks.

CONCLUSION

For healthcare organizations aiming to thrive in a sustainable future by embracing ESG principles, the work begins at the top with effective governance.

The benefits of leading ESG initiatives span improved patient outcomes, operational efficiency, the attraction of engaged talent, and long-term financial performance. By integrating sound governance frameworks and standards into their operations, healthcare organizations can position themselves as industry leaders—meeting stakeholder expectations, mitigating risks, and ensuring regulatory compliance. Recognition of the significance of ESG governance to create long-term value and contribute to the sustainability of their operations can make a transformative impact on both the well-being of individuals and the environment.

While the benefits of ESG-focused governance in healthcare can be substantial, healthcare organizations—notably, their boards—must address barriers to realizing those benefits. These barriers may include limited awareness and understanding of ESG concepts, insufficient resources and expertise, and resistance to change within organizations. Overcoming these obstacles requires investments in education and training, technological advancements, collaborations and partnerships, and engaging with industry associations and professional networks in healthcare to share best practices.

Healthcare organizations that recognize the significance of ESG governance can create long-term value, contribute to the sustainability of their operations, and make a transformative impact on the well-being of their communities.

ACKNOWLEDGMENTS

The author thanks Michelle Frazier, JD, CHC, CCEP, chief compliance and privacy officer, Advocate Health, and Laura L. Sak-Castellano, CPA, CHC, CHIAP, chief audit executive, Advocate Health, for their contributions to this article.

REFERENCE

Barton, D., J. Manyika, and S. K. Williamson. 2017. "Finally, Evidence That Managing for the Long Term Pays Off." *Harvard Business Review*. Published February 7. https://hbr.org/2017/02/finally-proof-that-managing-for-the-long-term-pays-off.

FOR DISCUSSION

1. Describe *sustainability* as it applies to healthcare operations.
2. Describe *corporate social responsibility* as it applies to healthcare operations.
3. What are some of the barriers to the adoption of ESG practices in healthcare?
4. How can those barriers be addressed? Who can address them?

Notes on Recognizing Risks, Prioritizing Responses

ATTILA HERTELENDY, PHD

SUMMARY

Healthcare organizations must play a leadership role in addressing environmental and social crises because those crises can have significant effects on the health of their communities.

Responses to environmental and social crises call for effective governance. In social crises such as poverty, unemployment, and inequality, this strategy can include the development of community health programs, partnerships with community organizations, and the incorporation of social determinants of health into healthcare delivery. Likewise, environmental crises such as natural disasters, heat- and pollution-related illnesses, and vector-borne disease outbreaks require vigilance, including risk assessment and the proactive development of emergency response protocols.

THE FOLLOWING LIST of best practices can help healthcare organizations prioritize a governance strategy to meet the complex challenges of social and environmental crises.

- Develop a mission statement that incorporates a commitment to addressing social and environmental issues.
- Establish a board committee or task force responsible for developing, implementing, and sustaining programs related to social and environmental issues.
- Incorporate social and environmental considerations into strategic planning and decision-making processes.
- Engage with community residents to understand and address their social and environmental concerns.
- Emphasize environmental stewardship by minimizing the carbon footprint and promoting sustainable practices in the healthcare organization.
- Measure and report on the organization's progress and impact on social and environmental issues.
- Identify local long-term implications of climate change and plan accordingly to meet the healthcare needs of the communities being served.
- Collaborate with other healthcare providers and community organizations to address social and environmental issues at a broader level and promote resilience and adaptation to rising challenges.
- Address health disparities that climate change creates or exacerbates, particularly among disadvantaged and marginalized populations. Incorporate social and environmental considerations into emergency preparedness and response planning, such as identifying vulnerable populations and addressing needs they may have during an emergency.
- Establish a mechanism for monitoring and assessing the likelihood and potential impact of identified risks.
- Prepare to respond to the increased frequency and severity of extreme weather events. Build relationships with local emergency management agencies and other organizations that may play a role in disaster response. Continuously

evaluate and improve disaster response capabilities and procedures.

- Develop communication plans that provide timely and accurate information to internal and external stakeholders during a disaster.
- Advocate for governmental policies and programs that address the root causes of climate change and promote social equity.
- Develop a risk management framework that identifies and prioritizes potential social and environmental crises such as natural disasters, pandemics, and social unrest.

PRIORITIZATION EXAMPLES

With best practices set in place, healthcare organization boards can support appropriate initiatives.

- A hospital in a coastal area or floodplain may prioritize natural disaster preparedness and response by developing evacuation plans and securing emergency generators to maintain power during an outage.
- A hospital in an urban area may address social unrest by developing plans for mass casualty events involving large crowds and potential civil disturbances.
- A hospital in a rural area may prepare to address disease outbreaks by developing plans for providing medical care and support to remote communities and identifying potential quarantine locations.
- A hospital in an area with a high amount of air pollution may prioritize environmental health issues by reducing emissions from its own operations and collaborating with local organizations to address air pollution in the community.

Boards that fail to recognize the risks posed by environmental and social crises and prioritize effective responses will likely face far-reaching consequences to their organization's reputation, financial stability, and ability to operate in the future.

Case Studies

Case Study
Stony Brook University Hospital: Working Cleaner, Smarter

CAROL A. GOMES, CPHQ, FACHE

SUMMARY

To protect the well-being of their communities and the planet, healthcare organizations must take the lead in correcting the negative impacts of their business on the environment by finding new ways to work cleaner and smarter. Stony Brook University Hospital has been recognized for committing to develop and maintain sustainable practices—from the elimination of mercury to the efficient design of new facilities—that are good for the environment and good for business. With the participation of the entire organization, from the C-suites to the front lines, the results are measurably impressive.

CONTEXT

An academic medical center with 624 beds, Stony Brook University Hospital (SBUH) serves as Stony Brook Medicine's tertiary and quaternary care center and regional trauma center for Long Island's Suffolk County. Stony Brook Medicine is also home to the Stony Brook Heart Institute, Stony Brook Cancer Center, Stony Brook Children's Hospital, and Stony Brook Neurosciences Institute. SBUH encompasses the county's only Level 4 regional perinatal center, state-designated AIDS center, state-designated comprehensive psychiatric emergency program, state-designated burn center, Christopher Pendergast ALS Center of Excellence, kidney transplant center, and the nation's first pediatric multiple sclerosis center.

Stony Brook Medicine's mission is to deliver world-class, compassionate care to our patients, advance our understanding of the origins of human health and disease, and educate the healthcare professionals and biomedical investigators of the future, so they can bring the fruits of scientific discovery to our patients. Specifically, SBUH pursues the three quality priorities of clinical outcomes, patient safety, and the patient experience, and builds upon the five strategic pillars of quality and safety, people, service, growth, and sustainability.

NEEDS

The primary responsibilities of healthcare providers are to heal and promote human health. Unfortunately, hospital operations can exert a significant negative impact on the natural environment with the wasteful use of energy and the application of toxic chemicals that have a direct effect on public health. Therefore, healthcare must take the lead in correcting and preventing this negative impact while also finding new ways to operate more efficiently and cost-effectively. Social citizenship and environmental mindfulness are important sustainability goals.

Stepping in the Right Direction

To begin its journey to sustainability in 2007, SBUH developed plans to become mercury-free. The first step involved replacing all lab and patient mercury thermometers, sphygmomanometers, mercury dilators, mercury switched-on fire pumps, mercury-containing reagents, mercury batteries, and mercury vaccines. As a result, SBUH gained recognition as a mercury-free hospital by Hospitals for a Healthy Environment, an organization founded by the American Hospital Association, American Nurses Association, Health Care Without Harm, and US Environmental Protection Agency (EPA).

This success led SBUH in 2009 to become the first hospital in the country to sign a "sustainability commitment" with the EPA to not only eliminate mercury but also reduce and recycle solid waste, cut energy and water consumption, limit regulated and chemical waste, create a more healing environment, and establish green policies.

In agreeing to this environmental policy, the hospital committed to promoting healthier communities, both locally and globally, and to be an environmental leader in all operations in a manner that protects human health. This effort catalyzed additional innovations to improve environmental performance through conservation, purchasing, and reuse/recycling.

Furthermore, SBUH established environmental responsibility as a corporate value with annual goals and action plans to continuously monitor, evaluate, improve, and report the quality and measurable outcomes of environmental programs.

SBUH's actions proved prescient. Shortly after the EPA agreement was signed, the governor of New York issued a requirement for state facilities to reduce energy use intensity by 20 percent, with 2010 data serving as a baseline year. These directives, in conjunction with more recent regulatory requirements, all support organizational efforts associated with environmental sustainability.

RESPONSE

To develop an organizational structure that could support sustainability efforts and achieve strategic goals, SBUH leadership decided to draw from the resources of Practice Greenhealth, an international networking organization dedicated to the transformation of hospital practices to improve the environment. The structure covers key areas identified by Practice Greenhealth: Engaged Leadership, Less Waste, Safer Chemicals, Greening the Operating Room (OR), Healthy Food, Sustainable Procurement, Energy, Water, Green Building, Climate, and Transportation. Led by me as the CEO/COO, the sustainability steering committee identified a stakeholder for each key area and subsequently formed teams to develop goals that contributed toward the overarching strategic plan for sustainability. Representatives from the departments of environmental health and safety, construction, physical plant, environmental services, supply chain/procurement, food services, facilities planning, the OR, pathology, nursing, and human resources have all served in leadership capacities to develop, implement, and monitor identified strategic objectives.

Each key area team meets monthly; the sustainability steering committee meets quarterly. The steering committee reviews strategic goals and objectives to determine whether a team is on target or requires assistance from senior leadership to address any barriers preventing it from accomplishing its objectives.

Gathering Data

In its first year, the sustainability steering committee became acclimated to the type of data required to monitor performance for environmental efforts. The committee identified baseline metrics such as percent hazardous waste, percent hazardous waste costs, total gallons of solvents reprocessed, solid waste average cost per ton, recycling waste average cost per ton, total pounds of waste per staffed bed per day, and hundreds of additional data points.

In sharing its baseline data with Practice Greenhealth, SBUH is able to benchmark its performance against other hospitals in the Practice Greenhealth network. The initial report provided a gap analysis to serve as a base for a strategic plan to address organizational and data-gathering needs. Key area teams review each section of the report and, following the feedback report, develop measurable goals and objectives for each year.

Early efforts revolved around the mechanisms to capture baseline data. For example, the Energy/Water Conservation team immediately sprang into action by submetering all buildings on campus to measure steam, electric, and natural gas use. Additional examples of projects to support energy conservation have included planned upgrades to heating, ventilation, and air-conditioning units. Air handler replacements were incorporated into annual and multiyear capital plans. A renewable energy master plan includes implementation of temperature setbacks for unoccupied buildings, units, and office suites.

Lighting, ventilation, and building management updates all have contributed to a decrease in energy use. For example, all ORs are now equipped with light-emitting diode (LED) surgical lighting to reduce energy consumption.

RESULTS

A large part of any hospital's environmental footprint is produced in the OR. At SBUH, recycling is a focal point for OR waste reduction, and efforts have been made to ensure that the staff puts used medical supplies in recycling bins. Purchasing of recycled medical devices is encouraged whenever feasible.

Also, the hospital has cut back on the blue plastic wrap used for boxes of sterilized surgical instruments by 30 percent in the past two years. This improvement has been achieved by switching to reusable stainless-steel containers and sterilizing instruments inside them. This cuts back on blue wrap and keeps instruments securely sterile in storage until they are needed.

To improve operational efficiency, the Greening the OR team collaborates with clinicians to review surgical case packs (kits of supplies organized by surgical service). The annual accounting and reporting process identifies instruments that are not being used and can be removed from packs to reduce waste. The team also collaborates with the hospital's primary implant vendors to reduce tray weights and shift to validated containers.

To eliminate the use of EtO (ethylene oxide) gas, a highly toxic sterilizing agent for surgical instruments, hospital leadership purchased sterilizing machines that use hydrogen peroxide, a cleaner and more efficient sterilizing agent. The Greening the OR team's multiyear effort recently culminated in the elimination of EtO from the OR environment.

A temperature setback initiative was introduced in existing OR suites and at the ambulatory surgery center to conserve energy. The design of two new ORs includes setback capabilities, which demonstrates how leaders are now incorporating environmental sustainability into their building and operational plans.

To highlight potential hazard issues that must be considered before acquisition and implementation, the department of laboratories created a checklist for managers to use when requesting capital equipment. The hazard analysis determines precautions for electrical safety and the proper disposal of hazardous waste and chemicals. In the core and histology laboratories, equipment that generates hazardous waste has been replaced with clean instrumentation.

In addition, chemical waste streams are evaluated periodically to identify new disposal options that may have less environmental impact. For example, as an alternative to incineration, laboratory xylene and alcohol waste is used for energy recovery (fuel blending), which means it is used as fuel for industrial processes. The hospital facilities team has moved to low volatile organic compound (VOC) latex paint, as well as VOC adhesives and sustainable plywood and medium-density fiberboard in furniture.

Partnering with the local fire department, SBUH recently coordinated a "Return Unwanted Medicines" event at the firehouse. Nearly 500 pounds of drugs were dropped off by more than 140 community members. In the wake of this initial success, the US Drug Enforcement Administration continues to conduct this event twice yearly at the same location.

Other pharmaceutical initiatives include a program to reduce unnecessary insulin waste throughout the hospital. Instead of dispensing one vial of insulin glargine per patient, the pharmacy now uses the hospital's automated dispensing machines with bar-coded labels to allow nurses to withdraw single doses of insulin for patients and label the individual insulin syringes at the dispensing machine. In its first four months, the project reduced insulin purchases by 77 percent, for an estimated annual savings of nearly $300,000.

Up on the Farm

One of the hospital's proudest accomplishments relating to sustainability is the creation of the Stony Brook Heights Rooftop Farm. Even with COVID-19 restrictions, the hospital was able to harvest nearly 1,300 pounds of farm-to-patient tray produce in its first season. Employees also participated in receiving local farm shares during summer and fall (Exhibit 1).

From 2016 to 2022, the food service department cut purchases of meat and poultry by almost one-half by decreasing portion sizes and substituting seafood and plant-based proteins such as beans, nuts, seeds, and soy. The hospital also promotes the use of tap water by providing bottle-filling stations for staff and visitors. Donations of excess food to local charities reduce waste (and food insecurity) as well.

With an eye toward environmentally responsible purchasing, the hospital's product management committee applies the following

Source: © 2022 Stony Brook University. Used with permission.

criteria to its decisions: (1) use less of a product, (2) conserve resources such as water, energy, and virgin materials required to use or produce a product, (3) eliminate or reduce waste (e.g., minimize packaging), (4) reduce toxicity, (5) consider recyclability, (6) compare functionality and effectiveness of choices, and (7) tally the total cost of ownership (i.e., unit cost, cost of waste). The committee also asks group purchasing organizations to provide details on purchasing attributes according to established agreements for reprocessing and recycling services.

In recognition of this comprehensive approach to sustainability, Practice Greenhealth has designated SBUH as an elite Top 25 Environmental Excellence Award recipient. SBUH also has received

Practice Greenhealth's Greening the Operating Room Award and Circles of Excellence Awards for waste reduction efforts several times.

These and additional results of environmental sustainability initiatives at SBUH are described in detail at https://www.stonybrook medicine.edu/sustainability.

Applications to Practice

Sustainability is a social responsibility, and the healthcare sector must accept that responsibility in meaningful ways by acting now to ensure a cleaner environment and reduce the waste that is generated at healthcare facilities. Although it may be true that environmentally preferential purchasing can contribute to higher costs, it is undeniably true that unnecessary waste exacts a high price as well. Reducing healthcare's carbon footprint is a necessity. As the SBUH experience illustrates, collective organizational efforts can make a difference in the quality of life on this planet.

Case Study
Guadalupe County Hospital:
Facing Unique Social Challenges

CHRISTINA R. CAMPOS, MBA, FACHE

SUMMARY

Social determinants of health (SDOHs) are the "conditions in the environments where people are born, live, learn, work, play, worship, and age that affect a wide range of health, functioning, and quality-of-life outcomes and risks" (Healthy People 2030 2021). These conditions include economic stability, education access and quality, healthcare access and quality, neighborhood and built environment, and social and community context. Ultimately, social determinants affect health status and outcomes to a greater degree than direct clinical care. Although these factors are experienced at a personal level, their impact can be seen on a community level. Also, while SDOHs vary, they tend to be more negatively impactful in rural communities—which then experience more harmful effects on health outcomes than their urban or suburban counterparts (National Advisory Committee on Rural Health and Human Services 2017). The unique experiences and challenges of rural communities require unique solutions. Guadalupe County Hospital in Santa Rosa, New Mexico, collaborates with community partners to address SDOHs. These efforts have a positive impact on their communities and can be replicated in other rural settings.

CONTEXT

Guadalupe County Hospital is a 10-bed acute care facility in Santa Rosa, on the eastern plains of New Mexico. The county's population of 4,452 covers approximately 3,000 square miles and is primarily Hispanic. The hospital was constructed in 1952 under the Hill-Burton Act. Through the years, the hospital has endured management turnovers, transitions, bankruptcies, and near closures. In 1999, the community established a local not-for-profit corporation, New Mexicare Inc., to serve as the governing board of the hospital on the county's behalf. This board's mission is not only to govern the hospital but also to enhance the community's quality of life.

The hospital's mission is to "provide compassionate and quality care to every patient, every time." It employs 50 persons, plus contracted clinicians, and provides inpatient care, emergency services, laboratory and radiologic diagnostics, pain interventions, and retail pharmacy services. The campus also houses an independent federally qualified health center (FQHC), the county's public health office, a private dental clinic, and a private pain intervention clinic that coordinates procedures with the hospital. As a governmental entity, the hospital is not required to complete community health needs assessments. However, it does so to identify and address needs and to improve the overall health of the community. The National Rural Health Association recognized the hospital as a top 20 rural community hospital in 2019, 2020, and 2021.

NEEDS

Economic Stability

Economic factors that affect health include employment status, income, and poverty level. These factors are interrelated, with unemployment or underemployment resulting in lower incomes and higher poverty. While poverty is usually measured at the household level, the social impact spans neighborhoods, counties, and regions. The result is communities of persistent poverty with inadequate housing, high crime and dropout rates, and poor health. All of these results limit economic opportunities and perpetuate poverty. In Guadalupe County, the average median household income from 2016–2020 (in 2020 dollars) was $31,061, in contrast to a national median household income of $64,994 (US Census Bureau 2021). The percentage of persons living in poverty in the county was 22.8 percent (US Census Bureau 2021).

Education Access and Quality

Insufficient educational opportunities result in fewer job opportunities and lower pay, thus leading to more poverty. While rural high school graduation rates have increased in Guadalupe County, they remain low. The US Census Bureau (2021) reported that the percentage of persons aged 25 or older with high school diplomas was 82.6 percent; but for a bachelor's degree or higher, Guadalupe County's rate was only 8.5 percent (compared to the national rate of 32.9 percent). The lack of college-educated persons presents a twofold challenge for Guadalupe County Hospital—the harm to health outcomes that result from increased poverty and lower health literacy and the shortage of qualified health and hospital workers.

Healthcare Access and Quality

There is only one location to apply for Medicaid coverage in Guadalupe County, which leaves many communities without convenient access to in-person services. While the ability to apply online for Medicaid or insurance through the Healthcare.gov Marketplace has improved access for most people across the United States, vast rural areas such as Guadalupe County do not have broadband internet. Furthermore, many patients must drive long distances to access primary, dental, mental, and emergency care and to pick up pharmaceuticals in Santa Rosa. With Guadalupe County's status as a federally designated Health Professional Shortage Area, the task of offering affordable and convenient healthcare is especially daunting—but doable.

Neighborhood and Built Environment

Currently, there are only two dollar stores, a few convenience stores, and one grocery store (which gets deliveries of meats, fruits, and vegetables just once or twice a week). In terms of housing, 16.44 percent of Guadalupe County households live in poor quality and/or unaffordable housing (Well Being in the Nation Network n.d.). Some homes lack complete plumbing, heating, or ventilation, many are crowded with multiple generations and extended families, and some cost more than 30 percent of a household's income. Access to safe, affordable, and adequate housing can improve well-being; conversely, poor quality housing can contribute to infectious or chronic diseases (through mold or wood smoke), injuries (burns, trips, falls), and poor childhood development (lead poisoning).

Access to safe parks and sidewalks also is an important factor for social determinants of health (SDOHs). Santa Rosa has numerous parks, sidewalks, paths, ball fields, and decent lighting, but most outlying communities in the county do not.

Social and Community Context

One SDOH that usually is positive for close-knit rural communities such as Santa Rosa is the strength of social and community relationships among family, friends, and coworkers. However, the social restrictions during the height of the COVID-19 pandemic put a damper on most gatherings at work, social, and religious venues. This resulted in higher levels of isolation, anxiety, and depression. The challenge is getting these structures back fully in place without endangering the health of the community with new outbreaks.

RESPONSE

Economic Stability

New Mexicare was established as a 501(c)(3) not-for-profit safety net for the failing hospital. The corporation provides governance and operational oversight for Guadalupe County Hospital through a management services agreement; its board of directors serves as the hospital's board of directors, as confirmed by the county commission. The board, like all hospital boards, is specifically responsible for strategic planning, quality and credentialing, financial oversight, and supervision of the hospital's CEO. However, this management structure allows the 501(c)(3) to charge for its governance services and to fund community initiatives that benefit the health and welfare of the community without violating the state's anti-donation clause for governmental entities.

Education Access and Quality

The first several years of the New Mexicare–Guadalupe County Hospital partnership were dedicated to stabilizing finances and general operations. By 2004, the hospital had healed to the point where the board could start working on broader community needs and concerns, including SDOHs. Most of these concerns were not new and the community had already made efforts to address them, but funds were limited, the focus was often short-term, and the results were mixed. For example, early on, the community recognized the need to address healthcare staffing through improved educational opportunities. In the 1980s, the local Rotary Club established a scholarship for nursing students to support the recruitment of both traditional high school graduates and nontraditional returning students. Initially, only one or two students were funded at a time, but the program nevertheless brought a handful of new nurses into the hospital. Beginning in 2004, New Mexicare assumed the nursing scholarship program and expanded it to include all health-related fields. Since then, New Mexicare has awarded more than $375,000 in scholarships. Today, more than 75 percent of the hospital's nursing, laboratory, radiology, pharmacy, and administrative staff is homegrown and educated.

Other community entities that have been able to hire graduates of the scholarship program include the state prison, FQHC, and the public school system. These health-related jobs are also some of the highest paying in the community, and efforts to further educate and gainfully employ our own citizens continue. Currently, the hospital has seven full- and part-time employees attending nursing classes. That is in addition to six recent high school graduates benefitting from the scholarship program. The hospital also provides tuition reimbursement for certification programs and continuing education in all hospital-related fields to maximize job satisfaction and growth opportunities.

Healthcare Access and Quality

With programs for developing a workforce well underway, the hospital board turned its attention to the aging facility. As previously mentioned, Guadalupe County Hospital was constructed in 1952. By 1999, it was barely meeting life safety code standards set by the Centers for Medicare & Medicaid Services, even with a multitude of building safety waivers. There was no doubt that the facility had to be replaced, as its construction and location did not allow for upgrades or expansion. In 2004, New Mexicare purchased several acres for a new facility. The land was then donated to the county to ensure that the hospital would remain a public, county-owned facility. New Mexicare and hospital leadership worked with county officials to secure a United States Department of Agriculture rural development essential facilities loan. The loan was secured with future hospital revenues and did not require new taxes or any county investment. The new hospital opened in June 2011, and the loan was paid in full in April 2021. As noted earlier, the new campus houses the 10-bed hospital, emergency department, diagnostic departments, private primary care clinic (now an FQHC), county public health office, retail pharmacy (now owned by the hospital), private dental clinic, and private pain intervention clinic. In all, New Mexicare contributed $460,000 for the land, architectural renderings, feasibility study, and landscaping.

Many other efforts to expand or maintain access have centered on provider training and recruitment, including financial support for medical students and medical residency programs. Currently, the hospital hosts medical students from the Burrell Osteopathic Medical School and family practice residents from the University of New Mexico (UNM) School of Medicine. New Mexicare has contributed more than $175,000 to the UNM Foundation to support the residency program. These partnerships have benefited the hospital and community by providing doctors who return to the community to work after their training. Three of the hospital's current doctors are from the UNM family practice residency program.

In 2018, New Mexicare purchased and renovated a house for physician housing. This not only supported physician staffing but also rehabilitated and beautified an iconic home in the community.

New Mexicare has provided funding for medical services to support the community, not just the hospital's operations. This commitment has included purchasing furniture and equipment for the dental clinic, providing start-up costs and equipment for the physical therapist, and awarding funds for provider recruitment for the local FQHC. Other local programs funded by New Mexicare include training for emergency medical technicians (EMTs) and certified nurse assistants for the assisted living facility.

The hospital and New Mexicare have joined with other providers and insurers to support yearly health fairs, too. These events offer free flu shots and blood pressure and diabetes screenings. In early 2021, during the height of the COVID-19 pandemic, the hospital and New Mexicare organized countywide free vaccination events. More than 900 persons were vaccinated in one day and later boosted. These events were staffed by the hospital, EMTs, and the county sheriff's office, and hosted by local schools. New Mexicare then made contributions to the county, the city, and the schools to support their health initiatives. Free COVID-19 vaccinations and boosters continue at the hospital.

Healthcare quality has been central to the hospital's success and stability. For several years, the hospital has partnered with the New Mexico Department of Health Office of Rural Health, the National Rural Health Association, and the National Rural Health Resource Center to identify gaps in care or finances and develop and implement quality improvement plans. Guadalupe County Hospital has worked with consulting firms to improve financial metrics in preparation for alternative payment models and to enhance the quality of care through patient experience, outcomes, and equity of care. Current projects are centered on discharge processes to reduce readmissions and ease transitions to home, as well as a health equity assessment to identify gaps in care and develop programs to close them. As these projects progress, New Mexicare plans to sponsor remote patient monitoring by the local primary care clinic, more outreach clinics for improved cancer screening, and more exercise and nutrition programs.

Neighborhood and Built Environment

In addition to its support of quality and access programs, New Mexicare has sponsored neighborhood and environmental programs like water quality improvement at the local swimming hole and spraying for mosquitos to prevent West Nile virus infections and other diseases. Other supported neighborhood programs include the local behavioral health council, the county health council, and the local community development corporation. Through participation in community development, New Mexicare has supported the Santa Rosa Main Street program's business development and downtown rehabilitation and beautification efforts.

Social and Community Context

While the large-scale COVID-19 vaccination events were offered to prevent disease, they were also the only opportunities for community residents to interact (albeit socially distanced and masked), when churches, community centers, schools, and many businesses were closed for several months. The biggest challenge at the vaccination events was not traffic control or staffing, but rather keeping folks at least six feet apart. Other social and community projects and events that the hospital and New Mexicare have sponsored are the community health needs assessments, the annual county fair and livestock auction (which supports educational scholarships), fishing derbies, bicycle rallies, farmers markets, and the restoration of the local movie theater for use not only for film viewing but also for county commission meetings and other public or private events.

RESULTS

Although Guadalupe County's population has declined 5 percent from 4,680 in 2000 to 4,449 (US Census Bureau 2021), access to health services has stabilized and, in some cases, expanded. While still financially fragile, the hospital building is paid for in full and maintained with well over a year's days of cash on hand. While nurse staffing remains a challenge, there are more physicians in the community now than at any other time in the hospital's history.

This financial and operational stability has allowed the hospital and its governing board to effectively address the county's SDOHs and improve the community's overall quality of life. Since 2004, New Mexicare has invested nearly $2.5 million in the community for education, facility construction, provider recruitment, health and prevention outreach, economic and community development, and social events. This does not include the contributions Guadalupe County Hospital makes to the health and welfare of the community, saving lives, and keeping people healthy.

There is still much work to be done—especially in outlying communities—to reduce disparities and improve the county's SDOHs. However, the private–public partnership between New Mexicare and Guadalupe County Hospital is a model that other communities might adopt to meet local needs and ultimately improve health.

REFERENCES

Healthy People 2030. 2021. "Social Determinants of Health." Updated August 2, 2021. https://health.gov/healthypeople /objectivesand-data/social-determinants-health.

National Advisory Committee on Rural Health and Human Services. 2017. "Policy Brief: Social Determinants of Health." Published January 2017. https://www.hrsa.gov/sites/default

/files/hrsa/advisory-committees/rural/2017-socialdeterminants
.pdf.

US Census Bureau. 2021. "QuickFacts: Guadalupe County,
New Mexico." Published July 1, 2021. https://www.census
.gov/quickfacts/fact/table/guadalupecountynewmexico,US
/PST045221.

Well Being in the Nation Network. n.d. "Housing in Guadalupe
County, New Mexico." Accessed August 18, 2022. https://
www.winmeasures.org/statistics/winmeasures/new-mexico
/guadalupe-county-housing.

Case Study
Chesapeake Regional Healthcare: Providing Support from the Top for Impactful Relationships

REESE JACKSON, JD, MHA

SUMMARY

When governing boards of healthcare organizations resolve to support their executive teams' commitments of time and money to create strategic action plans that meet their communities' environmental and social criteria—and when those healthcare organizations work with others that share their passion to measurably improve health—their communities can realize remarkable benefits.

For example, this case study describes Chesapeake Regional Healthcare's collaborative approach to a community health need that began with data from the hospital's emergency department. The approach included the development of intentional relationships with local health departments and nonprofits. The possibilities of such evidence-based collaborations are endless, but the support of a solid organizational structure is required as data collection identifies additional needs.

CONTEXT

Chesapeake Regional Healthcare (CRH) is a non-state-owned public hospital and health system serving southeastern Virginia. CRH and its partner organizations have been leading the charge to advance health equity and increase awareness of free resources to help area residents live longer and healthier lives. CRH's efforts toward effective environmental, social, and governance (ESG) action are informed in large part by the American Hospital Association's (AHA's) Health Equity, Diversity & Inclusion Dashboard (AHA 2020). It includes domains that reflect both an inward and outward focus:

- Data collection, stratification, and use
- Cultural competency training
- Diversity and inclusion in leadership and governance
- Strengthening community partnerships

Importantly, the dashboard links ESG to healthcare. It is based on race, ethnicity, and language data to identify the critical needs of patients as the first step in building community partnerships to address health equity.

The intersection of ESG and risk management should be noted. ESG includes risks that historically have not been factored into business practices. Today's major institutional investors expect publicly traded organizations to commit to ESG criteria and are viewing those criteria as material to long-term corporate performance. In the healthcare sector, rating agencies are beginning to reference ESG in their assessments of creditworthiness, while grant providers are accentuating equity, including health equity and social determinants of health. It also is possible, if not likely, that hospital accreditation standards for climate change and health equity will emerge from the widening interest in ESG. Fortunately, many opportunities exist for hospital governing boards and executives to apply ESG criteria in positive and humanistic ways.

NEEDS

CRH, in concert with the Chesapeake Health Department and its governing board, gathers extensive information from a periodic community health needs assessment. Data from the needs assessment in 2021 sparked the interest of a registered nurse in the CRH care management department. That inquiry led to a quality improvement research study that identified the demographics of patients who repeatedly visited CRH's emergency department (ED) for primary care. Many of these patients were middle-aged women from the 23324 zip code of Chesapeake where the population is primarily Black, mostly female, and includes many single parents. CRH researchers found that these residents experienced high rates of chronic illness but lacked access to medical care. Furthermore, many could not afford medical care (including medications), even with deductibles and copays, after making rent or car payments. They desperately needed more resources that could make a positive impact on their health.

RESPONSE

To address this situation, CRH leadership focused on its annual strategic operational plan, which is reviewed by the governing board in its annual allocation of resources. The annual plan includes goals and objectives for quality, growth, human resources, finances, and community. The CRH board's commitment to financial and human capital underscores several strategically important points:

- Sustainability programs require sustenance from the top.
- Needs assessments should be incorporated into the annual plan.
- Research methodology can lead to evaluative outcomes.

As a model of this corporate commitment to breaking down barriers to, and disparities in, care, CRH worked with its community partners to establish a wide-ranging program: Women's Wellness Wednesday. The program soon grew to welcome the whole family and shortened its name to Wellness Wednesday to emphasize the broadened inclusivity.

Wednesday every quarter, CRH teams up with more than 40 local groups and organizations to offer resources, information, vaccinations, and screenings to help improve the community's health. CRH's partners include the City of Chesapeake and its fire, police, and human resources departments; the Chesapeake School System; various nonprofits, including those that support LGBTQIA rights; legal aid societies; and Healthy Chesapeake, a state-supported 501(c)(3) created by CRH, the city, and the health department (Exhibit 1).

Among Wellness Wednesday's free resources are employment outreach (CRH has hired several attendees as associates) and food and childcare assistance. Screenings include mammography, blood glucose, blood pressure, A1C, vision, cholesterol, skin cancer, and hearing. Each participating organization contributes resources to cover these offerings. The health department administers flu shots and vaccines, CRH community nurses perform many of the screening tests, CRH registered dieticians provide diabetic education, libraries share books and laptops, and the Chesapeake Police Department offers an identification photo service. Locations for the event vary among churches, community centers, schools, and shopping centers in the at-risk area. Locations revolve and expand to ensure coverage of the entire population.

RESULTS

In a survey taken at the end of the first year of Wellness Wednesday, 80 percent of attendees noted improvements in their health. Specific results were impressive. Comparing data from the calendar year 2022

Exhibit 1: Wellness Wednesday: A Collaborative Corporate Commitment to Public Health

Source: © 2021 Chesapeake Regional Healthcare. Used with permission.

to 2020, ED utilization within the zip code trended downward significantly, along with an inpatient decrease of 10 percent and a 19 percent decrease in outpatient encounters. Other initial results included a 36 percent increase in cholesterol screenings, a 9 percent increase in blood pressure checks, and a 22 percent increase in COVID-19 vaccines. In addition, 77 percent of attendees said they made dietary changes because of what they learned at the event. And based on requests from area residents, CRH opened a community pharmacy.

Health Quality Innovators (www.hqi.solutions) recognized the program with its 2022 Innovator Award for health equity. This award recognizes organizations that have successfully implemented interventions to address disparities related to race and ethnicity, socioeconomic status, geographic location, disability, and/or sexual orientation across a range of conditions.

REFERENCE

American Hospital Association. 2020. "Health Equity, Diversity & Inclusion Measures for Hospitals and Health System Dashboards." https://ifdhe.aha.org/health-equity-diversityinclusion-measures-hospitals-and-healthsystem-dashboards.

Index

Abraham Lincoln Memorial Hospital, 133

Access to care, expanded, 77–78

Accountability: corporate social responsibility and, 146–147; for inclusive governance practices, establishing, 176, 178

Action Collaborative on Decarbonizing the US Health Sector, 26

Advancing Cities Challenge, 74

Advocate Aurora Health, 159–169. *see also* corporate stewardship in healthcare; board refreshment and diversity, 166–167; CEOs, 161, 163, 164–165, 167; data collection, health equity and, 165–166; directors, decisions and responsibilities of, 161–163; diversity, equity, and inclusion committee, 159, 162, 166; leadership principles, establishing, 164; management incentives, 166; mission statement, 162; summary, 159

Affordable housing, improving health through, 75–76

Agency, 78–80; cultural responsiveness, bolstering, 79; racism in the workforce, confronting, 79; representation in medicine, ensuring, 80

AHA. *see* American Hospital Association (AHA)

Air quality, 5

All About Adrian Resident Coalition, 115

American Hospital Association (AHA), 29, 36, 137, 201, 222

American Nurses Association, 201

American Society for Health Care Engineering (ASHE), 36–39, 40

Analytics tools, ESG, 185

Another Chance of Ohio, 120

Antibiotic-free food, 27

Ascension, 17–31; antibiotic-free food, 27; Better Buildings Challenge, 25; collaboration, 29–30; commitment to environmental sustainability, 18–19; "crawl, walk, run" strategy for data, 28, 29; energy efficiency data, 28; environmental impact and sustainability program, 19, 22–23, 27; environmental journey and milestones, 23, 24–27; FY 2021–2023 goal, 21; governance, 22–23, 24; green teams, 24; healthy communities, 17–18, 20, 22; impact investment strategy, 30; lessons learned, applications of, 27–30; net zero places, 17, 20–21; overview, 18; purpose statement, 19–20; Race to Zero campaign, 25–26; reprocessing and recycling single-use devices, 27; The Resource Group, 23, 26, 27; responsible supply chain, 17, 20, 21;

University of New Mexico (UNM)
School of Medicine, 215
UNM Foundation, 215
UNM School of Medicine. *see* University of New Mexico (UNM)
School of Medicine
UpTown, 114
URiM. *see* underrepresented in medicine (URiM)
USDA. *see* US Department of Agriculture (USDA)

Value, ESG for creating, 188–190;
capital, access to, 189; operational
efficiency, 189; patient and community engagement, 190; regulatory compliance, 190; reputation,
enhanced, 188–189; risk management, improved, 189; talent,
attracting and retaining, 189
Vector-borne illnesses, 5, 193
Veterans Administration Medical
Center, 46
VHA Erie VA Medical Center, 135

VOCs. *see* volatile organic compounds
(VOCs)
Volatile organic compounds (VOCs),
204–205
Vulnerable communities, focus on, 148,
149

Waste diversion, 26
Waste reduction, 13, 15, 139–140, 203, 207
Water contamination, 5
Water management, 49
Well-being: employee, 116, 155; patient,
183
West Nile virus infections, 217
White House/Department of Health
and Human Services Health Sector Climate Pledge, 147
Whole School, Whole Community,
Whole Child model, 99
Wildfires, 3, 5, 6, 7, 8, 30, 31, 49
Williams, Serena, 59
Witt/Kieffer, 173
Women's Wellness Wednesday, 223,
224, 225

About the Editor

Carla Jackie Sampson, PhD, MBA, FACHE, is clinical professor and director of the Health Policy and Management Program and online Master of Health Administration Program at New York University's Robert F. Wagner Graduate School of Public Service, where she teaches courses in strategy, executive leadership, human resources management, and healthcare system organization. Her research interests include healthcare workforce policy, the impact of structural racism on the social determinants of health, and anchor mission strategy development. She was coeditor of *Human Resources in Healthcare: Managing for Success*, 5th ed. (Health Administration Press, 2021). Carla received a master of business administration degree in healthcare management and a master of science degree in healthcare financial management from Temple University. She earned her doctorate in public affairs–health services management and research from the University of Central Florida, Orlando, and is board certified in healthcare management. Carla is a fellow of the American College of Healthcare Executives, for which she serves as editor of the quarterly publication *Frontiers of Health Services Management*, where articles in this book first appeared.

Note of Thanks
The editor expresses deep gratitude to Andrew Spencer, her former graduate assistant, for his help in finding these great stories.

About the Authors

Michele Baker Richardson, JD, is board vice-chair of Advocate Health and board chairperson of Advocate Aurora Health. She is also founder and president of Higher Education Advocates, LLC, and serves as a volunteer for The Leverage Network.

Denise Brooks-Williams, FACHE, is senior vice president and CEO of market operations at Henry Ford Health System in Detroit, Michigan.

Christina R. Campos, MBA, FACHE, is administrator of Guadalupe County Hospital in Santa Rosa, New Mexico.

Craig A. Cordola, MBA, MHA, FACHE, is executive vice president and COO at Ascension based in St. Louis, Missouri.

Michael J. Dowling is president and CEO of Northwell Health in Great Neck, New York.

Jonathan J. Flannery, FACHE, FASHE, CHFM, MHSA, is senior associate director, advocacy, for the American Society for Healthcare Engineering of the American Hospital Association in Chicago, Illinois.

Kathy Gerwig, MBA, is a strategic adviser on climate and health and was formerly vice president, employee safety, health and wellness, and environmental stewardship officer at Kaiser Permanente in Oakland, California.

Carol A. Gomes, CPHQ, FACHE, is CEO and COO of Stony Brook University Hospital in Stony Brook, New York.

Richard G. Greenhill, DHA, FACHE, is director of the bachelor of science in healthcare management program at Texas Tech University Health Sciences Center in Lubbock, Texas.

Antoinette Hardy-Waller, MJ, RN, is the founder and CEO of The Leverage Network, a not-for-profit that prepares Black executives for advancement to boards and senior leadership positions in healthcare. She is also a member of the CommonSpirit Health Board of Stewardship Trustees.

Attila Hertelendy, PhD, teaches in the executive MBA program at Florida International University in Miami, Florida, and in the international executive master of professional studies in emergency and disaster management program at Georgetown University in Washington, District of Columbia.

Reese Jackson, JD, MHA, is president and CEO of Chesapeake Regional Healthcare in Chesapeake, Virginia.

Merette Khalil is a consultant (hospital resilience) at the World Health Organization Eastern Mediterranean Regional Office in Cairo, Egypt.

Emily Kryzer, MSW, MPH, is the manager of research and evaluation with BJC HealthCare's Community Health Improvement Team in St. Louis, Missouri.

Janice G. Murphy, MSN, FACHE, is president and CEO of Sisters of Charity Health System in Cleveland, Ohio.

Monica L. Nakielski, ESG and sustainability adviser, is the former vice president of sustainability at Advocate Aurora Health.

Christopher M. Nolan, FACHE, is the director of anchor initiatives with BJC HealthCare's Community Health Improvement Team in St. Louis, Missouri.

Randy Oostra, DM, FACHE, is cofounder and managing partner of Blueprint Private Equity Fund and was formerly president and CEO of ProMedica in Toledo, Ohio.

Emily E. Wadhwani, FACHE, is senior director of U.S. Public Finance at Fitch, based in Chicago, Illinois.

Kate Walsh, former president and CEO of Boston Medical Center Health System in Boston, Massachusetts, is secretary of Health and Human Services in the Massachusetts Executive Office of Health and Human Services.

Suggested Uses in the Classroom

THE STORIES IN this book were originally intended to inform healthcare leaders. However, they can also serve as primers for a wide range of related topics such as anchor mission strategy development, health equity, community partnerships, and new approaches to healthcare delivery. Thus, this book is a valuable resource for healthcare management students because it presents contemporary environmental, social, and governance articles and cases that aid in honing problem-solving skills, applying theory, engaging in dynamic discussions, and developing practical experience in decision-making.

CASE METHOD

In an unstructured case method approach, the instructor assigns a case (a chapter of this book), and students read and prepare an analysis for class discussion. Open-ended questions are provided at the end of each chapter. The instructor can pose the questions either to the class or to specific students. A formally structured approach requires each student to prepare a written report using specific guidelines in, for instance, situation, background, assessment, and recommendation (SBAR) format. The instructor initiates a discussion by asking one or two class members to present their analysis.

Alternatively, the material can form the basis of an in-class debate based on the case method. This approach highlights how the range of stakeholder interests must be balanced in strategy. This activity will help students develop critical thinking skills, improve public speaking and presentation abilities, and learn how to work effectively in a team.

Before the class:

- **Students review the case.** They should identify the key issues, challenges, and opportunities to understand the scenario thoroughly.
- **Students are divided into teams.** Each team should have a clear position on the case and be prepared to argue in support of their position. Students may also be assigned a specific role or perspective related to the scenario (e.g., the CEO, a community activist, a board member, a patient, medical staff). They use critical thinking skills and consider the perspectives associated with their assigned role.
- **Debate team roles are assigned.** These team roles and responsibilities may include team leader, researcher, or speaker.
- **Research begins.** In researching the case, students gather evidence to support their team's position. They need to use academic literature, news articles, or other relevant sources to support their arguments.
- **Arguments are prepared.** Based on their research, students prepare persuasive arguments to support their team's position. Arguments must be logical, well-structured, and supported by evidence.
- **Practice makes perfect.** By trying out the presentation of arguments in front of their team and getting feedback from teammates, students can refine their arguments and improve their presentation skills.

Later, in class:

- **Debate begins.** During the in-class debate, each team should take turns presenting their arguments, carefully listening, and then respectfully responding to the arguments of the other team.

- **Evaluations are shared.** After the debate evaluation, students may be asked to identify areas for improvement and think about what they could have done differently or arguments they could have made, either in class or as a one-minute paper.
- **Plan to follow up.** Following up on the scenario and its implications in future classes, assignments, or projects will help reinforce the key concepts and skills learned through the case method.

Whatever the approach, students should be reminded to adopt a structured and analytical mindset to the question at hand. By categorizing the case's facts based on specific criteria such as organizational objectives and stakeholder expectations or interests, students can effectively organize them. This step will enable them to craft an accurate problem statement and identify the key issues. It is worth noting that developing precise problem statements necessitates teacher experience with the case method and some work experience in healthcare.

Carla Jackie Sampson, PhD, MBA, FACHE